Jen's Journey

Jennifer Carroll is best known for her Instagram page @jens_journey_ie, in which she documents her journey to healthier living. She lives in Tallaght with her son, Carter.

Jen's Journey

How I changed my life,
meal by meal – and you can too

JENNIFER CARROLL

GILL BOOKS

Gill Books
Hume Avenue
Park West
Dublin 12
www.gillbooks.ie

Gill Books is an imprint of M.H. Gill and Co.

9780717194933

Designed by Anita Mangan
Edited by Jane Rogers
Indexed by Eileen O'Neill
Printed and bound by the L&C Printing Group, Poland
This book is typeset in Quasimoda and Better Times.

This book is not intended as a substitute for the medical advice of a physician. The reader should consult a doctor or mental health professional if they feel it necessary.

Some names and identifying details have been changed to protect the privacy of the people involved.

The paper used in this book comes from the wood pulp of sustainably managed forests.

A CIP catalogue record for this book is available from the British Library.

5 4 3 2 1

For Carter, my forever purpose.
Without you, I simply would not be me today.
Mo ghrá, go deo.

Contents

Dinners

Introduction

Let's start from the very beginning, a very good place to start. For a long time, I thought writing a book would be a good form of self-help for me – almost therapeutic. And hopefully, it could offer some kind of support to the reader if they were in a place similar to where I was. But I want to make it clear from the beginning that I am absolutely not a professional or expert in any shape or form when it comes to diet and exercise. I just want to share my journey in as raw and as honest a way as possible, along with what I have taken from the professionals who have helped me along the way. I don't want this to be a 'diet book' or a 'how to…' because I really believe as individuals we all work differently, and what works for one won't always work for another.

THE SUPPORT FROM ALL ANGLES – SOCIAL MEDIA, FRIENDS AND FAMILY – WAS WHAT CARRIED ME THROUGH THE TOUGH TIMES AND ALLOWED ME TO OPENLY EXPRESS MY JOURNEY WITHOUT FEELING JUDGED.

One thing that worked for me and especially helped at the beginning of my journey was reading and hearing other people share their own experiences of situations they had faced that were relatable to me. The feeling of loneliness I felt throughout my journey is something that always stands out to me when I look back. Even when I was surrounded by the most supportive friends and family, there were still so many times that I felt very alone. I was struggling with things that nobody I knew had any experience of. So while having my friends to vent and talk to was always helpful, I also held back a lot. Having a platform on social media became a safe space for me initially. I was able to talk openly with strangers who were going through, or had been through, the same things I had or having the same thoughts and feelings as I had. There was no shame or worry of judgement, and it felt amazing to have that safety bubble to which I could escape.

The support from all angles – social media, friends and family – was what carried me through the tough times and allowed me to openly express my journey without feeling judged. It was so encouraging to me when I heard other people's stories, and it allowed me to see that I, too, could possibly help others feel the same way by sharing my journey as honestly as I could. So, hopefully, by putting my story out there in print, going back to the beginning and sharing a lot of what I've faced, grown from and learned along the way, I can show one person who maybe feels rock bottom right now that with the power of your own self-belief, commitment to yourself and consistency, you can turn your situation around. It was important to me to share not only my recipes and lifestyle tips that have worked for me but also my story. I chose the name 'Jen's Journey' for my social media pages because that is exactly what it is. It has never been a smooth road, and there are so many areas to cover when sharing this kind of story. Not just the meals that helped me get there but also the tears, the hard days, the negative thoughts and the shame. These are all a part of my journey, and they are all equally important.

I have always tried to remain as authentic to myself and to my journey as I can, even with my recipes. When I began my journey, I had a toddler at home and didn't have the time or money to cook what I would have then considered healthy meals. So, I worked with what I had and created really simple, achievable recipes that still allowed me to put my health first and achieve the goal I had at the time: to drop body fat. I didn't want my meals to be boring and bland, so I tried my best to make them a little bit more creative and something to look forward to at dinner time because it is important that we enjoy the foods we consume. In the past, when I was following a diet plan with very basic and repetitive meals, I would dread mealtimes and would always give up on a diet very quickly.

After trying hundreds of recipes over the last few years, I learned that a higher-protein meal worked best for me. I enjoy my three meals a day, along with snacks, so low-calorie and high-protein meals are ideal. This can change from time to time, depending on what I want to achieve, but when I had a lot of body fat that I wanted to drop in the beginning, I found that this method worked best for me and that a lot of my recipes naturally fall into that category. Of course, there are days when I want a higher-calorie dinner, so I have included lots of fakeaway recipes too, which I have used from the very beginning back in 2017. Every recipe is one that I've used myself. They're real meals with simple, tasty ingredients that don't require a huge amount of skill or cooking time. I hope you'll find them helpful as you begin your own journey.

My Journey

My body and me

As far back as I can remember, and as much as I hate to hear myself say it, I have had a very negative relationship with food and my body. I think the era I grew up in has a lot to do with it. I didn't know much about nutrition, and it wasn't spoken about very often at home or school. But diet culture and fat-shaming were everywhere.

DAD AND ME.

My friends and I couldn't walk into a shop without seeing tall, slim white women on the cover of every magazine, with article titles like 'She gave birth three months ago, but she is still HUGE!' and 'Who is the fattest female celebrity in a bikini this year?' We never bought into that culture or judged people the way the media did –

we would just roll our eyes and walk by – but it was everywhere. Seeing that daily, everywhere you go and even at home on the telly, is damaging for anyone, but it's especially damaging for young girls who think this is what they should look like. As an impressionable young girl, I really didn't have a clue about the importance of nutrition or a balanced diet, but I was very aware of the fundamental message that was constantly pushed in my face: that I wasn't good enough. I grew to believe it, which encouraged many unhealthy and dangerous choices in the years that followed.

AS AN IMPRESSIONABLE YOUNG GIRL, I REALLY DIDN'T HAVE A CLUE ABOUT THE IMPORTANCE OF NUTRITION OR A BALANCED DIET, BUT I WAS VERY AWARE OF THE FUNDAMENTAL MESSAGE THAT WAS CONSTANTLY PUSHED IN MY FACE: THAT I WASN'T GOOD ENOUGH.

I noticed from a very young age that I was always the bigger child at home or school. At home, my parents encouraged us to be active. We were always outside playing, running around or on our bikes. My brother was always at football, and I tried gymnastics for a little while. Swimming was the sport I loved to do most, but that love ended because I allowed the fear and shame I felt when I was in my swimming costume to overtake the joy that swimming gave me.

A LOT OF WHAT STARTED IT FOR ME, I BELIEVE, WAS ABSORBING THE LANGUAGE AND WORDS PEOPLE AROUND ME WOULD USE WHEN SPEAKING TO ME OR ABOUT ME.

My brother, who is two years older than me, was naturally very small and athletic when we were growing up. I have memories of being five or six years old and feeling uncomfortable that I had a larger frame than my big brother. On our family holidays as a young child, I would dread putting on a swimming costume in front of my family. It's sad that I grew afraid of it because of what I imagined others would think. I didn't realise it at the time because I was so young, but certain seeds were being planted that would programme my way of thinking about myself and my body for many years.

As toddlers, we can stand naked in front of the mirror and feel fabulous, oozing with confidence and smiling at what we see looking back at us. There is no other feeling, no negative thoughts towards our bodies, because that is all they are to us – just our bodies! Not our too-fat, too-jiggly, too-skinny, too-tall, too-short, too-pale, too-dark, too-dimply, too-ugly or otherwise not-good-enough bodies. But at some point, that lack of judgement stops. At some point, we start to develop those insecurities and negative thoughts and no longer smile at ourselves dancing in the mirror. We no longer see that pure freedom and confidence looking back at us. As I write this, my little boy is six years old, and it breaks my heart and scares me to think that one day he could lose the confidence and self-love he has for himself.

ME AGED 6.

A lot of what started it for me, I believe, was absorbing the language and words people around me would use when speaking to me or about me. For the most part, it wasn't done in a malicious way. Even when adult family members would comment on my puppy fat or talk about my diet in front of me, I don't think they ever thought it would be hurtful or would negatively affect me. But I did carry a lot of that with me. I sometimes mistook their worry for disappointment, but I think because I was so young, it was understandable that I was beginning to associate my appearance with feelings of failure. I wasn't good enough as I was, and I needed to change myself to look more like my friends and other children my age. It was as if I was beginning to be conditioned to think that I was bad or less worthy because of my weight.

My parents cooked us normal, balanced meals. We rarely had takeaways, and 'No sweets before dinner' or 'If you're hungry, have a piece of fruit' were common phrases in our house. We never went hungry, but we also never had the freedom to walk into the kitchen and dip into the biscuit jar as often as we liked. Looking back, I can see now that I was a normal, healthy, active child. The joy food brought outweighed the idea of getting fat. But by the time I was a teenager, I would tell my Mam and Dad that I was trying the cabbage soup diet or a no-carbs diet, and they never really intervened or realised how wrong it was. They were just trying to be supportive by saying, 'That's great, Jen. Let us know what we can do to help you.'

For as long as I can remember, food gave me a feeling of comfort and joy, as it does for many people – but we are often told that this is not a good thing. There is a difference, however, between the feeling you get from emotional- or binge-eating and the feeling of comfort and happiness that you get when you're truly enjoying foods you love. We make a lot of memories and traditions as families gather around the dinner table, enjoying special occasions together over food and drink. It is okay for food to be connected with a feeling of bliss and to be excited by or to look forward to eating.

It seemed very simple to me as a child: whenever I was sad, worried or upset, I would turn to the comfort of food. I knew that for a few moments, I could suppress those other negative feelings, which I didn't know how to deal with or speak openly about.

Just the two of us

One person that always made me feel one hundred per cent comfortable in my skin was my nanny, Annie McLoughlin. I have no memories of her ever commenting on my size or saying no to me when it came to food. I suppose some might even say my nanny was the person who contributed to my having a larger appetite. I absolutely adored and idolised her, and we had a really close bond. I

ME AND MY NANNY IN TRALEE IN 1998.

spent most weekends around the corner in her house, just the two of us, and I loved it!

I often felt that I was lucky to have my own mam as well as my mam's mam, who felt like a second mother. My nanny adored me just as much as I did her. I think she very rarely said no to me – even when I asked if I could snack on a block of cheese while watching our favourite film, *The Sound of Music*.

Nanny had Huntington's disease, and she slowly began to deteriorate from when I was really young. Her speech started going, and she couldn't walk very well, but her mind was still sharp, and her smile lit up my world. When I was around six, she moved into my family's house, and she and I shared a bedroom. I was absolutely delighted to have Nanny with me 24/7 – she was one of the very few people who enjoyed (I think?!) the dancing and singing shows I performed for them. I would have her hold my hand as I jumped around the sofa singing my heart out to 'Sixteen Going on Seventeen'. I'm pretty sure I asked her to do it even when she wasn't very sturdy on her feet, but she never said no to me! Every day after school, I would skip home, excited to see her and tell her about my day. She would always sit with a mug of tea and slice of buttered batch bread and listen to every word I had to say.

It took me a long time to see how unwell she really was. I remember when she could only get upstairs with my mam and dad assisting her. And then she had to be carried upstairs by my dad until, eventually, we turned our downstairs sitting room into a bedroom for her. I remember feeling sad because our sleepovers in my room every night had come to an end. But that didn't last very long because I would take my blankets downstairs most nights and squeeze into her single bed – my poor nanny! And when I was too big for that, I'd sleep on a fold-out bed beside hers.

But what stands out most in my mind about realising how sick she was, was that her appetite got smaller. I remember she would always give me half her toast or sneak me her biscuits as well as my own. Unbeknown to me at the time, it was probably because she couldn't manage it. Eventually, she would be fed through a tube. Even though I was young, I was eager to help and made sure I learned as soon as possible how to feed her. I would ask her every day what flavour of shake she wanted – not realising that she couldn't taste it! It was just another way to spend more time with my nanny and do what I could to help her and make her smile.

Eating to escape

During those years, from when I was around six to twelve, there was a lot of pressure on our family. My parents were both young, with two young kids of their own, and they were also my nanny's full-time carers. Looking back as an adult, I understand the strain it put on our family, but as a child, I couldn't understand why people were upset, frustrated or fighting. This is when I think I picked up two unhealthy habits: my emotional binge eating and my secret eating. I don't think it was as much of a problem when I was very young, but by the time I was a young teen, these habits were fully formed. I used them as a form of escape to help conceal my worries. I think I was worrying about things that were far too complex for a child to handle, and so hiding away in secret with some food became a huge comfort when I needed it. I remember being obsessed with food, constantly thinking about when I'd be eating again. I would repeatedly hear the phrase 'You eat to live, you don't live to eat', but I indeed felt like I lived to eat at times, and slowly it consumed most of my headspace.

My best friend, Aoife, and I would always be in each other's houses after school, and more often than not, when I was in her house, I would eat a second lunch or a first dinner. Her mam was an amazing baker and would make delicious cakes and desserts all the time, and I, of course, was delighted to sample her work. I would eat to my heart's content in Aoife's house and then go home and ask my mam what time dinner was – because I was starving! I started lying to my family regularly so that I could have extra food.

MAKING MY CONFIRMATION AGE 12.

The secret eating sometimes involved lying about what I had eaten that day at a friend's house. Other times, it would be grabbing something from the kitchen, running upstairs to my bedroom and stuffing it into my mouth as quickly as possible. I wouldn't even enjoy the food; it almost became a task of getting it into me as quickly as possible without anyone knowing and then hiding the evidence. Shoving the wrappers as far down towards the bottom of the bin as possible or leaving them in my coat pocket so that the next time I was out I could put them in a public bin. I wasn't sure why I did this; I think I just became a little obsessed with being in control of my feelings, and I

seemed to be able to rely on food for that feeling of comfort. Even now, when something bad happens or I have an argument, I often catch myself going to the kitchen and looking for the closest thing I can grab to quickly devour. It gives me a swift sense of reassurance and distracts me from whatever I'm trying to avoid.

ıı

I JUST BECAME A LITTLE OBSESSED WITH BEING IN CONTROL OF MY FEELINGS, AND I SEEMED TO BE ABLE TO RELY ON FOOD FOR THAT FEELING OF COMFORT.

ıı

But secret eating carries so much shame with it. I would basically hide away from people to eat because I was so ashamed of what I was allowing myself to do. I never wanted to be seen by anyone in that state. And over the years, I began to notice that I was doing it more and more regularly. I didn't need to be feeling worried or sad. There didn't always have to be a trigger to set me off. I would do little things like make a cup of tea for my mam and myself and scoff two biscuits while alone in the kitchen, and then walk into the living room with our tea and more biscuits and sit down and enjoy them with her. I think I worried that I would be judged negatively when I ate in front of people because I was a bigger girl – that seeing me eating would make them think about how much I must eat to get to the size I was. So, I would lie.

This was hard on my parents. I think I was doing it for so long and became so savvy that they couldn't figure out how I was gaining the weight, especially when my older brother was eating the same as me but not gaining weight the same way.

By the time I became a teenager, I hated eating in front of anyone. I had built that association between food and shame. During those years, I put on a lot of extra weight, and my self-esteem and confidence really started to suffer.

People-pleasing and paranoia

It's an awful thing to say, but I felt lucky in school that I was never badly bullied because of my size. There were plenty of occasions in and out of school where comments were thrown at me – and while I hated this, I don't think I fully realised at the time just how badly it affected me. Because of my lack of self-confidence, I was just grateful they didn't say anything worse. When anyone said something, I would just freeze and pretend like nothing had happened. I was always afraid to stand up for myself or say something back

because I knew they would just come back at me again. I'd rather stay quiet in the hope that they'd give up and leave it at the one comment. I always wanted to be liked and be someone's friend because, that way, it was less likely that they would comment on my appearance or make fun of me. I very quickly became a people-pleaser.

MY FRIEND NIAMH AND ME IN 2010.

When I walked into a room, I felt that people didn't see me – they just saw my size. So I created a loud, larger-than-life, bubbly personality that, I hoped, would show others that there was more to me than just my weight. I fell into a bad habit of making 'jokes' or derogatory comments about myself. My reasoning behind this was always 'I know everyone else is thinking it, so I'll break the ice and make it less awkward for us all by mentioning the elephant in the room.' I became the person who constantly made fat jokes, but it was always at my own expense. I built up a wall by saying the most awful things about myself so that if anyone else ever tried to say anything to me, I'd already have heard it or been called it. I think many people believed that I was this confident, bubbly girl, and had no idea of the insecurities and sadness I was hiding inside. I'm sorry that I allowed myself to think that way. I am sorry that I felt like I was less deserving.

One form of escape I always had was the theatre. I talk so much about struggling with confidence, so it's often a surprise to people that I love to be on stage because, for many people, that is the last place they would want to be. But for me, it was my escape. I was never Jennifer Carroll on stage; I was always in the role of my characters, telling their stories. I had good comedic timing, so I loved to play the funny characters and have everyone in the audience laugh along with me. This satisfied my need to please people, and I felt I was being seen for more than just my size. It became the role I took on in my personal life, too: the fat, funny friend. I hate that term because it is such a cliché, but I was that jolly girl. This persona I took on essentially became my comfort blanket. I didn't feel comfortable in my own skin, so it was easier for me to put on this act and feel more accepted.

Around this time, my friends and I reached the point where our little worlds revolved around boys. In school, it was always a topic of conversation: 'How many boyfriends have you had?' 'Who are you seeing?' 'Who have you dated?' I used to dread these questions. By the time I was 16 or 17, I felt like I was one of the only single people I knew, but I never put

myself out there when it came to boys. All my friends had been in serious, long-term relationships by this point. I hadn't had a serious or long-term relationship, and I was really self-conscious about it. I had conditioned myself to think that I was undesirable to anyone because of how I looked physically, regardless of what I was like as a person. For that reason, I never put any effort into boys.

I THINK MANY PEOPLE BELIEVED THAT I WAS THIS CONFIDENT, BUBBLY GIRL, AND HAD NO IDEA OF THE INSECURITIES AND SADNESS I WAS HIDING INSIDE.

If anyone did show me any interest, I would worry that it was a joke because I wasn't worthy enough to be approached. I became so paranoid, and people always told me how paranoid I was. This was frustrating for me, as there were so many occasions when I would see people look in disgust at me or whisper to another person. I could spot it a mile away, which made me paranoid about anyone who looked my way. I felt angry a lot of the time.

In my twenties, social media was becoming part of our everyday lives.

Capturing special moments and nights out with friends to share on our favourite platforms was slowly becoming the new normal … and I hated it! I'm sure many of us can relate to the fearful experience of waking up after a night out, seeing that you had been tagged in photos online and quickly scanning through every picture to ensure that they were okay before texting your friend to ask them to take the pictures down. It started with our pink neon digital cameras getting whipped out throughout the evening, but soon it became our camera phones. Once we all had smartphones, it was almost impossible to have a night out without getting snapped a few times – or, even worse, captured on video. I feel lucky that I wasn't part of the generation growing up today, with the enormous pressure that social media can have on young children, teenagers and adults. A little ironic coming from me, I realise, considering that social media is a big part of my job. Over the years, social media has held many positives for me. Still, there are unavoidable negatives too, and there are definitely days when it is easy to allow that to consume you. I think that because I speak so openly about how my body has changed over the years, my struggles with confidence and my body image, that is naturally what others will give opinions on. It can be difficult to read other people's opinions on your body when it is something you have struggled with for a long time, but I try not to take social media too seriously and remind myself to take everything with a pinch of salt. The most important thing to me is that I stay open and honest and

create the content I enjoy.

But back in those first years, when camera phones were pulled out, I became like a ninja. I could move as quick as lightning when I saw somebody whip out their camera. Dodging pictures became a talent of mine. I would excuse myself swiftly, explain why I should take the picture or just run for cover.

There were plenty of occasions when I would be out and, after a few drinks, would get loose on the dancefloor. I loved to dance – I still do. When I was out with my friends, I couldn't help myself, and they would be my biggest cheerleaders, egging me on. I remember, one night, I was in the middle of letting my hair down when I saw some girls standing next to us. Two of them had their phones pointing in my direction. I made eye contact with one, and she quickly turned and put her phone away while the other girl carried on sniggering and pointing. My heart sank, and I felt like the biggest fool in the place. None of my friends noticed, and I didn't dare tell them because the last thing I wanted to do was draw more attention to myself. I knew I'd get the usual 'Ah, you don't know if they were looking at you' or 'Maybe they thought you were good' or 'You're just being paranoid'. But I knew, in my heart, exactly what was happening. And for the rest of the evening, I stood still, watching my friends all dancing and laughing without a care in the world. As they should have been. Meanwhile, I was caught up in my own thoughts: *Am I so big that I look ridiculous when I dance? What if they send that video on to people I know or post it online and I become a laughing stock? Maybe I should go over and let them see that I'm a nice person and then they'll delete it for me? I'm never dancing again … I hate nights out.* I was so triggered by being the butt of their joke that I allowed it to ruin my whole night out with my friends.

"

IT'S A HORRIBLE FEELING: KEEPING YOUR HEAD DOWN AND TRYING NOT TO MAKE EYE CONTACT WITH STRANGERS FOR FEAR OF WHAT THEY MIGHT SAY.

"

That wasn't the first time. I have seen people take pictures or point phones at me on nights out, eating in a restaurant, sitting on public transport or at the beach. If it's happened to you before, you just know when it's being done. It's similar to when someone is whispering to their friend about you: you can sense it. I never wanted to react, retaliate or question them for fear of being more humiliated or ridiculed for getting angry and defensive about it, especially in public. So instead, my thing was to give them a sad smile, so they knew that I was aware of what they were doing and perhaps to make them feel a little bit guilty. I wanted them to know that I had feelings and was hurt by

what they were doing. A lot of the time, when I responded this way, they would look a little embarrassed, put the phone down and smile back.

But most of all, I hated being ridiculed in front of my friends. It was humiliating, and I worried that they would retaliate on my behalf. So often, I said nothing or would pretend I didn't hear a snide remark or rude comment, but my friends weren't as well trained as me when it came to keeping quiet over that kind of thing. Their reaction always came from a place of love, and I knew how much they cared for me, but when they stood up for me, I was always worried that it would cause a commotion and make more people look in our direction, and I would end up feeling even more humiliated.

Before going out, I would constantly harp on about how awful I felt and looked. I know I annoyed my friends with it. I'm sure it was draining for them to reassure me that it would be a great night and that I looked lovely. Each of them would always look great heading out, and this just fuelled my belief that I had the role of the fat, funny friend. There were occasions when someone made a joke or comment about my weight and everyone laughed instinctively, including myself – either out of embarrassment or out of not wanting others to feel uncomfortable. I especially hated being around drunk people at the end of the night. I was always tiptoeing around, trying not to get noticed, because I was such an easy target. It's a horrible feeling: keeping your head down and trying not to make eye contact with strangers for fear of what they might say.

All the while watching your friends laugh without a care, knowing that they never have those ridiculous worries that I put on myself. I envied that so much.

I could probably write a book alone about the number of uncomfortable situations I've been in because of my size. Some of them were caused by myself, and others were caused by people around me … or furniture! I have broken or cracked my fair share of chairs, beds and toilet seats. When I lived in London, I became a frequent flyer, coming back home to Ireland to visit throughout the years. And over time, these visits became less and less frequent simply because I didn't like the worry and the strain I caused myself. From start to finish, the whole journey was always stressful and something that I would be thinking about weeks in advance.

I would walk through the entire process over and over again in my head, thinking about all of the scenarios. Quite often, these scenarios would be ridiculous and not something that would ever occur. But simple things like my journey to the airport would be a huge worry. London is one of the best cities in the world for transport, with trains, tubes and buses all taking you directly to the airport. Still, all I could think about was being seen in public struggling to carry cases on and off trains, looking out of breath. I also had a constant fear of tripping in public (I still have that one!).

Going through the security gates once I arrived at the airport was something I hated. I would make sure I was wearing nothing that could possibly set the detectors off and make someone have to come over and pat me up and down while an entire airport of people watched (I know nobody would be looking, but this is how my mind worked). I would plan my outfit a long time in advance. For a few years, I had an airport outfit: a baggy black top with a lightweight black cardigan and leggings, with runners that I could slip on and off without bending down to tie laces. Winter was the best time for me – because I could wear my massive black coat that would cover everything.

I feared being late because I hated the idea of rushing and getting all hot and bothered, so I always arrived everywhere with plenty of time. I hated sitting around in airports on my own because I wouldn't eat alone in public. More often than not, it would be breakfast or lunch time before a flight, and I would be hungry. But I had this irrational fear that if I sat there eating alone, everyone who walked by or looked at me would be judging me.

I HAD A WHOLE ROUTINE I'D WORKED OUT OVER THE YEARS FOR COVERING UP THE SEATBELT THAT DIDN'T FIT ME.

Queuing for the plane was the worst part. I would have so many thoughts running through my mind. *Who will be*

sitting next to me? What if they're big too? Will I fit up the aisle with my carry-on? Will I fit in the seat? Will they ask me if I want a seatbelt extender when I'm boarding the aeroplane? I had a whole routine I'd worked out over the years for covering up the seatbelt that didn't fit me. I can remember my first flight when the belt didn't fit me; I was horrified. The fear of waiting for take-off and seeing the flight attendant walk down the aisle, checking every single seatbelt individually to ensure it was closed. I was with my friend and was too embarrassed to tell her. I was only about 20, and I couldn't believe it wouldn't close while I watched my friend tighten theirs with plenty of belt left over.

After we landed from that flight, I spent the entire trip worried about the return journey and the seatbelt. I always booked myself a window seat so I could shove myself up against the window as tightly as possible. I would be numb with pins and needles from how close I had pressed myself up against the window just to make sure that I wasn't bothering the person next to me. I would take my cardigan off before taking my seat and hold it in my lap. I'd place the seatbelt across my lap with the buckle on display and then carefully place my cardigan on the other side of the buckle to hide the fact it wasn't closed. When the flight attendant walked down the aisle to check the seatbelts, I'd stare out the window or close my eyes and pretend to be asleep, hoping they wouldn't notice.

It worked every time except for one flight back to London. I followed my usual airport routine, and everything was going

smoothly. I was almost through the hard part and was waiting to board the plane. As I stepped onto the plane, I was greeted with a smile and a question: 'Seat belt extender?' I shook my head, looked down and almost pretended I didn't hear what the flight attendant had asked. I took my seat, mortified. I wondered if anyone else had noticed what he asked me. As the plane filled up, I tried my best to avoid eye contact with him and everyone else on the plane. I set myself up in my seat and did my usual routine of extending my seatbelt and my perfect placement of the buckle. I held my cardigan tightly in my sweaty palms and turned my head to focus out the little window. It was almost time to take off, and every minute that passed brought me closer and closer to feeling relaxed and safe in the clouds. As the cabin crew members were coming down the aisle to complete their inspection, I heard, 'Excuse me, excuse me!' As much as I wanted to bury myself in my seat, I looked up to see a crew member walking towards me and swinging a bright orange belt extender in the air. 'I have an extender for you!' I immediately felt like he was trying to humiliate me.

In the rows ahead, I saw a few curious people look back to see who needed the extender. I must have stared at the attendant for a couple of seconds because the man beside me gave me a nudge and nodded towards the bright orange belt still swinging in front of me. I didn't know how to react, so as I reached out to take it, I pretended to be surprised and confused, as if to say, 'What is this contraption that I clearly don't need?' and then smiled and said thanks. I attached it to my seatbelt as quickly as possible while the man next to me watched. I told myself I was never flying again. But I did – with even more fear than before.

These scenarios now seem so over the top and ridiculous, but this was how my mind worked. Every event held the possibility of being a spectacle. My paranoia grew and grew. I was obsessed with my size and constantly worrying over every little thing and what other people were thinking. Over the years, as I got bigger, it got worse. Things like walking to the shops or answering the door. Looking back and seeing how much time and energy I wasted worrying about what other people were thinking (or not thinking) makes me sad. It also makes me realise that I was more self-obsessed than I had thought!

I WANTED TO BE LIKED BY EVERYONE, EVEN PEOPLE I DIDN'T PARTICULARLY LIKE MYSELF.

To avoid these situations as much as possible, my people-pleasing – a trait that had flourished since I was at school – became even worse. I wanted to be liked by everyone, even people I didn't particularly like myself. But some people can see this trait in you and take advantage. They could probably smell the

desperation off me a mile away, and they knew that if they told me to jump, I'd ask how high. I would accept poor treatment from people because I had been conditioned to think I was bad because of my weight. There were definitely a few a**eholes who made fun of me – but I allowed myself to think that everyone felt this way towards me. My mind was so engulfed with those thoughts – the feelings of shame that I'd picked up from the media, careless family comments and the few instances of genuinely malicious bullying I'd suffered at school and since – that I believed everyone thought of me the way I thought of myself.

I'm sorry I allowed myself to think that way. I'm sorry that I felt like I was less deserving. I'm sorry I didn't allow myself to do what I wanted. I'm sorry I said no to things because I worried it would make other people uncomfortable.

Plus-size rails and sucky-in pants

I started to say no a lot as I was approaching adulthood. I became so accustomed to saying no to things that I've missed out on so much. I've missed out on parties, holidays, experiences and relationships – all because I held myself back. I remember going on my first holiday with my friends to Lanzarote. We had just finished our Leaving Cert, and it was our first holiday abroad on our own. I was really looking forward to letting my hair down and celebrating with my friends, but in the back of my mind, I was constantly worrying about being in a hot country where it would be hard to hide underneath my usual black baggy clothes. I hadn't been away on a holiday like this before with friends, so as crazy as it sounds, none of them had seen me in a swimming costume. But I was proud that I said yes and agreed to this holiday as a once-in-a-lifetime experience with my friends.

> **MY FRIENDS WOULD THROW ON A SMALL BEACH DRESS OR A PAIR OF SHORTS AND A BIKINI TOP, WHILE I WOULD BE COVERED FROM HEAD TO TOE – MORE THAN LIKELY IN ALL BLACK, TOO – IN THE BLISTERING HEAT.**

I still held back, however, and missed out on things like going for a swim. Instead, I just sat by the pool, covered up with a kaftan, and watched the girls have a ball in front of me. Even things such as walking to the beach or to the supermarket weren't pleasant for me because I was constantly worrying about what I would wear. My friends would throw on a small beach dress or a pair of shorts and a bikini top, while I would be covered from head to toe – more than likely in all black, too – in the blistering heat. All because I had that little voice in my head constantly telling me what other people would think about me.

The evening time was an especially nerve-racking time for me. I remember watching the girls get dressed up in pretty, colourful summer dresses, belly tops and shorts – all looking fabulous. I would feel like their overweight, covered-up aunty taking them on a night out. I always craved the freedom that they seemed to have, to just feel attractive, confident and carefree walking down the street.

For women – especially teenagers and young adults – fashion is a huge part of self-expression and identity. But you need the confidence to wear what you want, and I never had that. Most people I knew could walk into any shop and pick something straight off the hanger. Growing up, I never experienced shopping like this; I would go straight over to the baggy, oversized clothes and look for the largest size I could find. I never dressed how I wanted to dress. I dressed my body to cover it up. Shopping for clothes was not something I enjoyed, and it was something that I very rarely did. When I was growing up, plus-size ranges were not a thing. There was one store with a plus-size range, and I hated going in (this was in the days before online shopping). I only ever went with my mam because I was too embarrassed to go with my friends. The options they had were very limited and not the same styles my friends would be wearing. Growing up, it seemed like size 8 to maybe 16 was all that was available in most shops. I wore things until they were literally worn out; I would only go shopping for jeans when my jeans had holes in them – which was more often than you would think because of the auld 'chub rub'. Special occasions and nights out were really hard to dress for because I wanted to look and feel as good as my friends did. On nights with the girls, I had maybe two or three go-to outfits, and I would wear those clothes every single time we went out. I would be so embarrassed because my friends would all be decked out in a new outfit every time. I do remember a couple of statement pieces. My beloved black bolero and leggings. I had always hated my arms and legs and was incredibly self-conscious about how big and broad they were. My bolero and leggings meant that I could pick up a couple of cute dresses and wear them all together. Unfortunately for me, this trend didn't last too long, but I dragged it out for as long as I could. Fashion really is supposed to be creative, fun and a brilliant way for us to express ourselves through colours, patterns and styles. For so long, I was so ashamed of my body that I didn't dare to dress it the way I wanted to.

I didn't think my body deserved the bright colours or pretty materials. I was always told by everyone to dress for my shape. They would say the same thing: big handbag for a big girl, belt to show you have a waist in there somewhere, avoid horizontal stripes, low cut to distract from your stomach, don't draw attention to your biggest areas and always long but never tight.

And then there was the sucky-in-pants phase. I was always told that they would transform my body in a second and that a dress would look ten times better on me if I just looked a little smaller. I would be more attractive with a smaller and smoother silhouette, like the tall slim women advertising them. By the age of 19, I had stopped believing that I would become the woman in the advert with the help of Spanx.

But there was a big change on the horizon. In a new country, maybe everything would be different.

ME IN 2017.

London

That period in your late teens and early twenties is such an important time of growth and discovery of who you are – but I never really got to be myself completely. For so long, I had been playing so many different versions of myself to suit the people around me that I had no idea who I really was. But eventually, I decided that moving to London with Aoife to pursue acting was what I wanted to do.

CHANGING MY MINDSET ABOUT HOW I SPEAK TO MYSELF IS ONE OF THE HARDEST THINGS I HAVE EVER DONE.

I began to see it as my big escape, a fresh start where I could finally work on discovering who I really was. I kept imagining a life where I didn't need to live a lie anymore, where I didn't need to feel like a failure or as though I was bringing shame and embarrassment to my family, friends and myself. My friends and family never gave me any reason to feel ashamed or like a failure, but I was almost 19 years old and was the heaviest I had ever been, and I felt like I had zero motivation to get up and change that. I had no idea of the kind of career I wanted, and the jobs I was working were simply jobs to get me by. Most days, I would have feelings of self-hate, shame and quite a lot of feeling sorry for myself. The only way I could describe it was like being in a constant state of melancholy. I had zero drive and zero respect for my health or my body. My life was beginning to feel like a constant game of 'What excuse can I come up with next to say no or to get out of this?'

I was at the age when people told me that the world was my oyster, but I was comparing myself unfavourably to everybody around me. Even though we were in completely different places in our lives, I always felt like I was the one stuck in a rut.

Looking back, what I find so disappointing is that all my worries and sadness were because of my weight. How did I allow myself to become so obsessed with feeling like less of a person that I needed to hide from friends and family and run away to another country, all because my frame was bigger? But I had this voice in my head from as far back as I can remember. It would constantly remind me of how fat I was, how ugly I was, how disappointing I was and how I should second-guess every little thing before I did it. Over the years of listening to my thoughts, I really did become my thoughts. We spend so much time with ourselves – more than anyone else in our life – that we trust that inner voice. We develop certain beliefs as young children, and as we grow older, it becomes so much harder to switch them off or change how we speak to ourselves. I had already wired my brain so that every single response was a negative one. I can't even remember a time when I said to myself, 'Well done, Jen' or 'I believe in you'. Changing my mindset about how I speak to myself is one of the hardest things I have ever done. I am still learning; I still struggle and fail at times; but working on unlearning how my brain worked for the last 30 years and rewiring it to work how I need and want it to work has been one of the greatest things I've ever done for myself. Positive thinking and self-love are superpowers that we can all learn – with a huge amount of effort.

MY FRIEND AOIFE AND ME AT HER HEN PARTY IN CARRICK-ON-SHANNON IN 2016.

The time finally came when Aoife and I were leaving for London. Seeing how sad a lot of our friends were that the two of us were leaving, and seeing my mam and dad get upset that their baby was flying the nest, was tough. I asked myself, 'Am I running away from my problems?' I wasn't addressing the issue of my weight by moving away. Still, somehow it felt as if I would be less ashamed there, as I only seemed to be getting heavier. Hiding in another country definitely seemed like an easier option than facing the real issue.

Highs and lows

My first year in London was one of growing up and having fun. Aoife and I moved in with a friend of hers, Georgie. I couldn't have asked for two better housemates; the three of us instantly clicked and never stopped laughing, crying or singing from the day we moved in together until the day we moved out. We experienced so many of our highs and lows together.

All of our first jobs over there were far from what we wanted, but they paid the bills. I got a job as a supervisor in a newsagent. The hours were awful: I started at 5 a.m. to get the paper deliveries ready. Telling myself that it was only temporary, to get me by as I settled into my new home, got me through it. I finished at lunchtime and headed home to an empty house, as the other girls usually didn't get home until later in the evening. As the weeks passed, I found myself in a really unhealthy cycle. I never had breakfast before going to work, so once it got to about 8.00 a.m. I would help myself to a snack off the shop shelf and eat it quickly while there were no customers around. I still didn't like to eat in front of other people, so I wouldn't bring lunch with me. I would wait until I finished work at 12.30 p.m. and then pop into the fancy delicatessen next door and treat myself to a pesto and mozzarella panini with some overpriced crisps. It became one of those situations where the man behind the counter knew my order and would have it waiting for me at 12.35 p.m. on the dot every day.

I ALWAYS FELT LIKE I NEEDED TO EAT UNTIL I FELT WHAT I THOUGHT WAS FULL, BUT REALLY IT WAS JUST BINGE-EATING UNTIL I FELT SICK.

We lived on a street at the top of Sydenham Hill, which is one of the highest points in London. I took the bus home, which would take me to the bottom of the hill, so I would get off, cross the road and wait for a second bus to take me one stop up the hill and leave me at the end of our road. I'd be embarrassed travelling just one stop, as it was pretty obvious that I was struggling to walk a few minutes uphill, so I had a whole performance down to a T.

I would get a 'call' just after I got on the bus, from someone explaining to me that they were at the previous stop and so I would need to get off at the next stop to meet them.

I HAD WANTED THE OPPORTUNITY TO CHANGE MY LIFESTYLE FOR GOOD AND TO COME HOME TO IRELAND ONE DAY AND SHOCK EVERYONE WITH MY TRANSFORMATION. BUT IT WASN'T TO BE.

As soon as I got into the empty house, I'd plonk myself on the couch in front of the television and watch marathons of *Grey's Anatomy* or *Sex and the City*. I'd usually have stopped in our local shop on the way home and picked up some extra junk food. Large sharing bags of crisps, chocolate to beat the band and always diet fizzy drinks. This is where I continued the secret eating. I would lie on the couch for three or four hours, exhausted from my early start and long shift, shovelling food with very little nutrition into my mouth and leaving myself feeling even more lethargic. Most days after eating that banquet, I wouldn't even feel that full. I always felt like I needed to eat until I felt what I thought was full, but

NIAMH, AOIFE, ME AND EMER IN 2020.

really it was just binge-eating until I felt sick. Before the girls arrived home, I stuffed all my empty wrappers and packaging into one plastic bag, squeezed it up tight, tied it and put it in the bottom of the bin. They'd never know.

I enjoyed cooking, so I would normally start dinner for us in the evenings, even pretending to be starving to the girls when they came in. This continued for weeks. I knew it wasn't how I wanted to live, and it wasn't why I had moved to London. I had wanted the opportunity to change my lifestyle for good and to come home to Ireland one day and shock everyone with my transformation. But it wasn't to be.

I continued working in the newsagent for another six months. One of the men I worked with was overweight and probably the biggest person I had ever encountered at that time. He was bossy, grumpy and an oversharer. Over time, he started to bring things up about my weight. I think he felt comfortable talking about his size and just assumed that I did too. But then he began to say things like 'You must understand' or 'It's hard for us' after he made comments about his size. I was always mortified when he would make these kinds of remarks and a little hurt too. Even though I was so aware of my size, when others commented on it, it was like a reminder that when people looked at me, all they saw was my size. One time, when my colleague was telling me about his holiday, he stopped mid-sentence and looked me straight in the face and said, 'You must have to book two seats too when you're flying, do you?' I couldn't believe that he had the nerve to ask me that kind of question and that he thought I was large enough to fill two seats. He went on to ask about seat-belt extenders and told me how he had bought himself one online to save the embarrassment of asking for one on the plane. He told me that if I booked priority, I could board first without having to struggle up the aisle. For the remainder of my time working there, plenty of conversations went just like that. I remember being so embarrassed by what he had said to me that I didn't even speak to my friends about it. I hadn't really experienced an adult male speaking so openly and freely about my body before.

When a person insults you or tries to hurt you with words, don't take that on. In that moment, you get to decide how much value and weight you will allow their words to have on you. Their opinion does not matter to you if you decide that it does not matter. Listen to it, take it in and then decide what space they will take up in your head. I wish I had done more of that with him!

Surviving

We spent the first year in London immersing ourselves in acting workshops, singing lessons and attending all the shows we could. Towards the end of our first year, I picked up a small job working alongside Aoife in a children's traditional toy and clothing boutique. It was around this time that we began preparing ourselves for drama school applications.

Auditioning for certain drama schools in London can be a tough process, and I know that anyone who has auditioned will agree with that. It's especially so when you're 19 years old. At almost every single audition, we were given the same advice: go and get some life experience. I had always been at my most confident when I was on the stage performing, but going through the gruelling, competitive rounds of auditions in London brought on my impostor syndrome. I was constantly comparing myself to everyone else in the room, questioning myself about why I was there. I would immediately forget my past achievements and doubt my ability to be as good as anyone else. I felt like a fraud. I constantly told myself that I was a joke.

The size that you are – and you want to become an actor? How often do you see serious actors of your size? You only ever did well in drama because you were the fat, funny one, not because of any real talent. I began to have these types of thoughts going through my head at every audition. It didn't help being stuck in a room with 50 other young women who were mostly slim, tall and stunning. *Why would they ever choose you for the next round?*

And so I began to lose the only small bit of passion I had. Acting had been my special escape and had given me the only tiny bit of confidence I had in myself. Why was I allowing myself and my thoughts to sabotage it?

" I HAD CONTROL OVER NOTHING EXCEPT FOR WHAT I PUT IN MY MOUTH.

"

After two or three years of auditioning with little to no luck in getting through to the final stages, I began to panic a little. It wasn't so much that I was concerned about not being where I should be or not doing what I should be doing. When you're in that kind of environment, surrounded by theatrical and creative people, there's less of that social pressure

that you must have A, B and C ticked off by a certain age or in a certain order. I was panicking because I was more concerned about how people from home would view me at my age with still not a degree or career in sight. Most of my friends were graduating from college, were at the beginning of their careers or were moving across the world. I felt like I was failing again – failing at the dream I had so openly shared with everyone. A part of me already wanted to give up on drama school out of fear of facing failure year after year. But what else was I going to do? This was the only thing I had ever wanted to do and the only thing I ever really believed I was good at.

I began to lie about small things, like getting a recall for an audition or filling out university applications and being proactive with workshops and auditions, because I felt as though I was failing at my own life. I wanted my family and friends to think that I was doing well and was perfectly normal and successful. But I felt like I was losing control of my dreams. I had no real concept of what I wanted to do. I didn't even dare to dream; it was all an unrealistic fantasy that would never be achievable. I felt undeserving and completely pathetic when I looked at my life and day-to-day routine. I had control over nothing except for what I put in my mouth.

Food always made me feel happy in the moment, and this was a comfort that I always went back to. But food never satisfied me. I always felt as though I had an insatiable appetite, and this would lead me to binge. I wasn't dealing with any of the doubt or unhappiness that I had inside, so instead, I focused on filling this void with food.

Heartbreak

On a positive note, when I was 22, I moved up a little bit in my job. I became the assistant manager at the children's shop for a couple of months while my manager was pregnant, and she was training me to take over as a full-time manager. I was delighted to let my parents know I was doing okay for myself. Being able to say that I was no longer solely focused on drama school auditions – because I had landed myself a decent-enough job for the time being – made me feel like less of a failure.

I sort of just sailed through life for a little while. I didn't apply to drama school at all that year. My social life started improving, and I had a good close circle of friends at home and at work. Aoife had moved to LA by this time, but I impressed myself with how well I was doing without my sidekick. It was still tough, as we had been like sisters since we were four or five years old – we had grown up on the same road together, gone to school together and moved to London together. We had gone through everything together and were each other's biggest support systems, but I was so proud of her for moving to California on her own to chase her dreams. Georgie and I still had each other and had grown incredibly close over

the previous couple of years. We moved out of our first home into a new house between Camberwell and Brixton. And I was incredibly happy to never have to walk up that hill again!

Georgie and I weren't long living in our new house when I got a phone call at work from my dad to let me know that my nanny had passed away. Those 48 hours were some of the toughest of my life, and they all seem to be a blur now. I remember my colleague at work helping me book a flight home. I couldn't even speak to Mam or Dad on the phone because I was in such shock. I remember my colleague putting me in a taxi home with a grey rabbit teddy that we sold in the shop. She gave it to me and said, 'Hold on to this until you get home. You'll be fine. Just keep squeezing him.' And I did, and I still have (well, Carter has) that teddy today.

MY MAM AND MY NANNY.

I remember packing for the trip home. I knew that I needed an outfit for the funeral, but I had nothing nice or new or remotely smart. I remember feeling awfully guilty that I wouldn't look presentable for my nanny's funeral. I had always wanted to make her proud. Every time I went home, I would have this heavy feeling of pressure in my chest – a fear that everyone would be so shocked and disappointed when they saw me come off the plane. I don't remember very much of that trip home; all I know is that after it, my visits home became less frequent.

As soon as I landed back in London, the emotional eating took over for a little while. I stopped socialising, had no interest in doing pretty much anything and was only really leaving the house for work or a food shop.

I always have felt, and still do, like I need to defend my diet. When people would talk to me about my weight or my diet, or when I opened up to friends and family about struggling with my size, I was always told the same thing: 'Stop eating so many takeaways!' When you're tipping the scales at almost 30 stone, I think most people assume you live on takeaways and junk food, but I could probably count on one hand the number of times I ordered a takeaway just for myself when I was living in London.

I do remember ordering takeaway pizza for myself not long after flying home from my nanny's funeral. I was feeling miserable and very sorry for myself. It was a Saturday night, and I had the house to myself, so there was no worrying about other people judging me for what I

ordered (even though they never would, but I was still paranoid). I decided that I might as well order a huge amount of food because, from Monday, I would be changing my lifestyle. I'm not sure if other people do this too, but any time I ordered a takeaway, I would shout out something like 'I'm getting the door' or 'Where did you leave the money?' when answering the door because I was worried about what that delivery driver would think of this big girl ordering so much food. I wouldn't want them to think that I was alone. From the moment I ordered the food until it arrived, I would worry about this and imagine different scenarios that would *never happen*! I always questioned my sanity when I wasted so much time thinking about these things – like, did my brain work the same way as everyone else's? Was it normal to think in this way, or was I just so obsessed with my size that I related everything back to it?

My daily diet really wasn't that bad. I've always enjoyed cooking, and over the years, with all the house-sharing in London, I usually took on the mammy role. I loved making meals from scratch for everyone at home and seeing their faces light up when they were handed a nice home-cooked dinner. My favourite evenings were the ones where we would all sit around the table talking and eating good food. Most of my dinners were cooked from scratch, but where I struggled with my diet was my secret eating and emotional eating. I would normally eat lunch alone, and this was usually a lazy, convenient lunch followed by huge amounts of crisps and chocolate – there was always a secret stash of those in the house.

"

I HAD BEEN FED UP A MILLION TIMES BEFORE, BUT I FELT REALLY FED UP WITH EVERYTHING THIS TIME.

"

But this is why my weight was always confusing to people who knew me. When they saw what I ate, it was relatively healthy and not what someone would expect from a person my size. I would say all the time, 'I've no idea how I'm gaining so much weight. I eat just the same as you in a day.' But I was in denial about how much I was eating secretly, and it was usually in a binge state, so I wouldn't even realise how much food I was consuming. People around me never knew how much or what I was eating because I never let them. I had perfected secret eating and organised my eating times around my housemates' schedules so that I could fit my extra meals in before they got home.

After months of what seemed like the same routine – the same crappy feeling, the lack of energy, the denial, the lying, the excuses – I was fed up. I had been fed up a million times before, but I felt really fed up with everything this time. I was spiralling out of control. I was deeply unhappy and wanted to change that, so I reminded myself of why I moved to London: I wanted to study and train in drama. That was my passion and my escape and what made me happy, so I decided that that was what I was going to do. I had got so caught up in the job that I was in, and I had just got comfortable.

At that point, it was too late in the year to apply for the autumn intake, but I promised myself I would submit the applications for next year as early as possible and work hard to make sure that the following September I was doing something for myself, something that I had wanted for so long. I was also happy that it would be almost a year before I would be starting any kind of course, giving me loads of time to lose all my weight.

This was a thing I always did. I think lots of us do it, but putting ridiculous pressure on yourself to make huge changes in a short amount of time is never a good idea. I was already telling myself that I couldn't start this course until I changed my appearance because I wasn't good enough as I was and wouldn't be accepted. I was applying to do a course in which charisma, creativity, stamina and acting skills are the most important, but I was already doubting my ability and trying to think of ways to change because my body wasn't good enough. This wasn't a new way of thinking for me, so at the time, I wouldn't have recognised – like I do now – how wrong I was and the message I was sending myself by thinking this way. I always came back to the belief of not being good enough as I was.

The romance

Things were going well at work, and I hired some new staff members. We were all around the same age and lived in the same area, so our work life and social life naturally began to merge. I had a new circle of friends with whom I spent most of my time, and it was through one of my colleagues that I met my ex-partner. I'm going to call him Eric.

Eric would often pop into the shop for a catch-up with his friend when he was passing by. He was good-looking, with a slim frame but built. It was from here that we started speaking a little. He was really quiet and came across as shy. I remember the first night we all went out together. Eric barely spoke to anyone. He just sat in the corner and looked like he was on his own. Even though we were all around him, he was minding his own business and taking everything in. We didn't talk much that night. I felt a little intimidated in his presence.

But after that first night out, he added me as a friend on social media and sent me a message to ask how I was. I wouldn't say it snowballed romantically from there. Even after talking for weeks, I was still unsure of him. He was hard to read and often hard to get anything out of. We could talk for several days and then have no contact for a few days. It was an act he played well. I think it drew people to him more and kept them intrigued.

Over the following few months, we hung out in our group and on our own. I enjoyed his company, and we had a very similar goofy sense of humour. That was what attracted me to him. He had a thick English accent, and at times we couldn't understand each other. Our casual back-and-forth 'friendship' went on for what felt like forever. But it was comfortable and easy.

> "
> ## IN MY GUT, I THINK I ALWAYS KNEW THAT HE WASN'T THE BEST PERSON FOR ME.
> "

Our mutual friend had said to me that we were not well suited and that they didn't see Eric and me ending well. But I didn't listen; I was a little infatuated and excited that someone I was attracted to was showing an interest in me.

In my gut, I think I always knew that he wasn't the best person for me. I knew he had dreams and things he wanted to achieve, but he had a bit of a 'poor me' mentality, like the world was always against him, so he was never motivated to realise these aspirations. I introduced him to the close circle of friends that I lived with, and it was nice to have all my friends mixing. But Eric was always shy and quiet when he was around them, and sometimes it was awkward when there were more than three or four of us in a room. He would often have a drink and then begin to relax and ease into the conversation.

I was never someone who had a drink at home in the evenings. I was always more interested in eating than drinking. Don't get me wrong – I love to go out for drinks and a dance, but I was never one to have a glass of wine while sitting in and watching the telly, so I didn't understand that he needed to have a drink when we were just sitting and chatting at home.

I didn't see Eric very drunk until maybe a year into knowing him. I had seen him get tipsy, but that was it. One night, I was staying at his, and he had gone out with an old friend. When he came home in the early hours, he was in such a state that I was shocked he had managed to make it home. At the time, it was funny to me. I took videos of him to show him the next day. All he could manage to do was laugh and then fall into bed. I thought he must have had a good night, but I could never imagine allowing myself to get so drunk that I couldn't stand. The idea of being so out of control of myself and my actions had always freaked me out. It would be another while before I saw him that drunk again.

Uni days

I kept my promise to myself and applied to some universities in and around London to study drama. I would be 23 when I started, so I was officially a mature student. I filled in all the applications, and I did my auditions. I completely faked my confidence throughout the entire process – and it worked. Sometimes, when you don't have that confidence, you have to fake it till you make it! This would only work for me temporarily; truly building or rebuilding your inner confidence requires a lot more work. But it helped a little with my impostor syndrome.

> **I COMPLETELY FAKED MY CONFIDENCE THROUGHOUT THE ENTIRE PROCESS – AND IT WORKED.**

At one university in particular, I felt a really good rapport between the interviewers and myself. It was the only audition where I wore a special chain that my mam had given me just after my nanny passed away. The chain had my nanny's wedding ring that she had left me on it. I never liked wearing it because I was afraid of losing it, but that day I decided to wear it for good luck, and it made me feel as though she was a little closer to me. For the first time in a long time, I felt confident in my talent and my performance. This university was also the closest to where I was living at the time and had a good reputation for the arts.

I was so proud of myself when I got my acceptance letter to Goldsmiths University. It was a small reminder that I was so much more than how I saw myself and how I thought others saw me and that if I put my mind to something and worked hard, I deserved to be there just as much as anyone else did.

CARTER AND ME DUETTING.

I knew I wouldn't be able to have a full-time job while studying, so I started looking for something part-time. I had felt a small sense of security with my management job and hated dipping into savings to pay for rent, bills and day-to-day things, so I wanted to land a job as soon as possible. There was an arts centre and theatre just a five-minute walk from the university that I thought would be perfect, so I applied there first and got myself a job.

My new job involved working in the theatre café and bar and reception and doing front of house. The hours were far less sociable than they had been in the shop, and I worried that I probably wouldn't have much time for my friends or for Eric. I remember feeling disappointed by his reaction to how excited I was about starting university. He kind of chuckled and reminded me that it was just a drama degree. Instead of getting annoyed, I felt a little guilty and thought, *Oh, he's probably jealous that I'm starting a whole new chapter*. He was just a little jealous that I was chasing what I wanted to do. But it was belittling to laugh at me. Despite that, I was just so excited to begin this new chapter, and for the first time in a really long time I felt as though I was accomplishing something for myself and was proud that I didn't I allow myself to hold myself back.

Of course, there were all the expected nerves and worries that come along with new beginnings, maybe even more so for me than for other people since I was a professional worrier at this point. As my course got closer and closer to starting, I was disappointed that, once again, I hadn't managed to drop the 10 stone I had planned to. But I was hopeful that all the rehearsals and running from uni to work and home again would encourage a more active lifestyle, which would be the kickstart I needed. I finished up at my old job, and it was a hard goodbye, as my colleagues and I had grown close. I had been so content there, but the change was a little easier to adapt to because so many things were changing at once. I started my new job a week before I started uni, which turned out to be a good distraction. The atmosphere in the theatre was very relaxed and welcoming. I started in the café, mainly doing day shifts. There was a vast, fully equipped kitchen, which meant we got to learn different skills. Every month, the café would base the entire menu around a new country, a guest chef would come in, and we would watch them cook their native foods. We all got to work alongside these different chefs every month, which was a great experience.

I KEEP MY MEALS AS SIMPLE AS POSSIBLE BUT NEVER BLAND.

I've always enjoyed getting a little creative with meals. At home, my dad was definitely the one that enjoyed cooking dinners the most. He would always cook at the weekends and was never afraid of unusual flavours and trying new things. He was never one to follow a recipe but would always come up with his own really tasty curries, pasta sauces, crazy salads and the best Sunday roast dinners around. So growing up, we definitely had a broader palate than most, and I think this is why I have never enjoyed 'boring' dinners. I keep my meals as simple as possible but never bland. Spending time next to such creative people in the kitchen at work by no means made me a professional chef or anything of the sort, but it allowed me to

watch them play with different flavours and foods. I would pick up some inspiration and small tips and tricks here and there, and I would always try to incorporate some creativity into my meals. I've always maintained this, even when losing weight – food doesn't have to be repetitive and boring! I may have changed portion sizes or the method of cooking, but I always maintained the flavours and experimentation.

We got our meals given to us at the café, which meant that I was saving money and time at home by not having to prepare meals for work. But it also meant that it didn't take long for me to pick up lots of unhealthy habits in terms of what I would eat each day. It was tough when you were already so concerned about your diet and trying to drop weight to be surrounded by such nice foods all the time.

I'VE ALWAYS MAINTAINED THIS, EVEN WHEN LOSING WEIGHT – FOOD DOESN'T HAVE TO BE REPETITIVE AND BORING!

My first term at university came around very quickly. The first day was so daunting; we sat in the theatre, and even though I was only three or four years older than most of the other students, I felt ancient. There were a few that were older than me too, but so many of them seemed younger. I felt painfully shy. What made it harder was that most of the people in my class were not from London either and had just moved down for university, so they were all living in student accommodation. A lot of them were being supported by their parents and didn't work for the first while or at all. It felt difficult to strike up new friendships as I wasn't living in the student accommodation, and when I wasn't in class, I was at work. I only lived a 30-minute bus ride away, however, so I tried my best to make an extra effort to show up to nights out and meet-ups when I could. The theatre setting also helped to break the barriers. After a while, I slowly started to build relationships with a few of the other students and felt more comfortable as time went on.

One thing I was constantly worried about was the physicality of the course. Drama involves so much movement, and it can be very physically demanding, with lots of exercises to rid you of feelings of anxiety. Even the thought of these exercises would give me anxiety. At this point, my body was the biggest it had ever been, and it had been a long time since I had done anything demanding or fast-paced. I worried a lot about not being able to keep up.

On the days that we had rehearsals, our attire was to be black, comfortable clothing. I was comfortable with this and picked up some black leggings and many oversized black tops. It would be a few months before we had one of our bigger productions on stage in front of an audience. But it wasn't being in front of an audience that I was worried about – it was the costumes for the productions. I didn't have a clue who I would be playing or even what I would be performing in, but I knew that someone from my class would be working in the wardrobe department and would need to take my measurements. It was easy for me to say no or be difficult with my nearest and dearest when it came to situations that made me feel uncomfortable. Anyone who knew me knew not to ever buy me clothes, ask me to take part in a fancy-dress theme, invite me to swim or ask me to pose for photographs (especially not on my own). I had absolutely no problem with saying no when it came to keeping myself hidden and deflecting attention. But it was different when it was a stranger asking – and my classmates weren't even strangers, just people who I wasn't entirely comfortable with. I never wanted to draw attention to myself by being difficult or problematic, and I especially didn't want to draw any extra attention to my size.

But when it came to things like costume changes, costume fittings or workshops that involved a lot of physical partner work, I would get on with it. But, of course, me being me, I constantly ridiculed myself and made jokes about my size every time I was in one of these situations – which basically did exactly what I didn't want to do: draw attention to myself. Often someone might find whatever joke I was making about myself quite funny, and that would almost convince me that it was okay to make them. But for the most part, my classmates would stop me with words of encouragement and compliments about how lovely I was and say that I shouldn't put myself down like that.

There was only one incident that really upset me at university. It happened in the first few weeks, when we had a special guest teach a movement class based on improvisation. She had a good reputation and had come over from France for a few weeks to work at our university. We were all excited to participate in her workshop, and the class was divided into smaller groups so that our time with her was a bit more intimate.

I don't remember too much from the class, but she told us that for most of her lesson we would work in pairs, and some of the exercises required you to be in a pair with someone of a similar build. I instantly felt my palms get clammy as I looked around the room, while also trying to keep my head down and not make eye contact with anyone. Nobody of my size was in the room, and I certainly wasn't approaching anybody out of pure fear that I would insult them. So I stood there, helpless, in the hope that maybe someone would realise how uneasy I looked and would offer out of sympathy. But it was too late. Most of the room was paired up, and the teacher saw me standing there, looking uncomfortable, so she walked straight up to me and said, 'You can just go with him,' and pointed to the tallest guy in the room. Luckily, I knew him well enough at this point and he would have had no idea how awkward I felt. I did wonder how the exercise was going to

work; yes, I was big and he was tall, but he was about 6 ft 3, and I'm only about 5 ft 5 on a good day. So the difference in height alone looked like it was going to make things a little clumsy.

The exercise was to sit back-to-back with our shoulders touching (already pretty impossible for us!) and push into one another, using that pressure to lift our bottoms off the ground and then back down again to the ground. The teacher kept reassuring us that our weight did not matter, and as long as we were both applying the same pressure, we would be able to lift each other up. I didn't have too much faith in this. I thought that I was going to crush this poor fella or send him flying.

I could see the teacher walking around the room, inspecting everyone. As she was getting closer to us, she kept glancing over every time we fell over, and I could sense her frustration. She came over, stood directly in front of me and said, 'This isn't going to work. Your new partner is the wall. You can work with the wall until this exercise is over.' I remember my entire body getting hot, and I got that horrible lump in your throat that instantly triggers your eyes to start filling up. I was humiliated.

My partner tried to convince her to let us try again, but to no avail, and I went over to the wall. After that workshop, I went to my class rep and explained what had happened. I couldn't hold my tears back when I told her how it had made me feel. I would never usually do that, because I'd want to bury it and move on, but I was glad I did, and my rep handled it really well. There weren't many other incidents like that during the rest of my time at uni, but I was proud that I had spoken up for myself. Defending my size wasn't something I usually did. But this was important for me, because everyone is entitled to feel comfortable, especially in an education setting.

Self-sabotage

After a few months, I finally got myself into something of a routine. The days went by so quickly, and I felt like I was always on the go, from home to class to rehearsals to work. We had rehearsals on the weekends, and I worked a lot of weekend nights too.

I REMEMBER HAVING THESE SILLY THOUGHTS AS A CHILD THAT I COULD WISH A YEAR OF MY LIFE AWAY AND JUST WAKE UP IN A NEW BODY.

I was on the go so much that I wondered why I wasn't dropping weight. I definitely had more energy because I was moving more, but, if anything, I was getting bigger, slowly but surely. I thought that

perhaps it was down to my diet: I rarely ate at home and wasn't cooking very often. My lunches were usually in a café or a meal deal from the supermarket, and there were always plenty of snacks being grabbed because I was constantly moving from place to place. By the time my shift would start in the evening, I wouldn't have much energy, so I survived on convenience foods and snacks that were handy at work. At the end of the day at the café, I would binge on the uneaten food that was going to be thrown out. On my breaks, I would go into the back room and scoff whatever I could get as fast as possible. I didn't want people to see me eating crap, and I was aware of how poor my diet looked at the time.

My housemate Georgie and I could not have been more different when it came to nutrition and health. Even after living together for years, we were at opposite ends of the spectrum. She had the healthiest diet of anyone I had ever known and was the only person I knew at the time who could eat two squares of chocolate and be satisfied, wrapping the rest of the bar up and putting it back in the fridge for another day. Georgie was a huge support to me when I wanted to cry my eyes out about how low I was feeling and when I was telling her every other week about the next juice cleanse or diet I was going to do to drop the weight. She never once judged me and only ever encouraged me and partook in whatever crazy diet I was trying at the time. She always reminded me that I was lovely as I was, and if I wanted to change, then that was great too but it made absolutely no difference to anyone what size I was. I was lucky that I had so many good friends that I could talk to, but sometimes it was still a very lonely place. I was always the only big girl. I was also always conscious of sounding like a broken record to them and aware that it might be frustrating or draining to hear me talk or complain about the same thing over and over.

FROM THE AGE OF ABOUT 18 OR 19, I STOPPED GETTING MY PERIOD EVERY MONTH.

I remember having these silly thoughts as a child that I could wish a year of my life away and just wake up in a new body. Or that someone would invent a type of chocolate that, for every piece I ate, I would lose a pound! Not the kind of things you should be wishing for as a child. I was afraid of the hard work that losing weight involved, and I was also afraid of failure. What if I couldn't ever succeed? What if I only ever got halfway and then I stopped, or what if I lost it all and then gained it back? I was so focused on the what-ifs and negative outcomes that I would convince myself that trying wasn't worth it. My time would come when I was ready, and then I would do it. On the other hand, I would spend so much time

regretting not starting a few years earlier. If I had just been more disciplined with myself in my teenage years, then I wouldn't have as much weight to lose. I should have tried harder – and so I would go on and on in my head, beating myself up and hating myself for being a failure. It's no wonder that I was never successful in changing my lifestyle: I was my own worst enemy. I didn't believe in myself and constantly put myself down, telling myself that I wasn't good enough and I never would be.

At this point, I was probably at the peak of my sensitivity when it came to discussing weight. I understand that there are so many opinions on the right and wrong ways to approach this when it comes to friends and family, but it is really hard to know how best to do it. We are all individuals, and our responses will be individual too. From being a parent now, I know that it must have been incredibly hard for my parents to see me get bigger and bigger over the years. They saw the effect it had on my confidence, my moods and my mental health. Luckily, my weight hadn't led to any illnesses up to this point. Still, I'm sure they were concerned that if I continued how I was going, I was opening myself up to possible health risks or complications.

From the age of about 18 or 19, I stopped getting my period every month. I could go a full year without one, and then there might be a sporadic month when it would arrive. I never told anyone about this because I was terrified of what it meant and also deeply concerned that it was irreversible. When I was in London a couple of years ago, I spoke to my GP about it. They said that this can happen to women for a number of reasons and that it didn't necessarily signify a serious problem, but that my weight could definitely be a factor in why my periods had stopped. I was to track them over the next year and return if there were no changes. My periods didn't come back, and I didn't go back.

When I began taking the contraceptive pill, it was a progestin-only one. One of its side effects was that it could stop periods altogether, so I would tell myself that that was why they weren't coming back. But I kept this information to myself for years, and I shouldn't have. It was always hanging over me, and I was worried about the damage that could be done the longer I left it. But I just couldn't face being told that this was happening because of my weight. I allowed myself to bear the burden of that thought for years. Instead of asking for help, I had almost accepted that my periods would never come back and perhaps I would never become pregnant. I wish I had spoken to my mam about this, because she would have supported me and gone wherever I needed to go for answers by my side.

Of course, it is not the case that being overweight equals being unhealthy. Anybody of any size can be unhealthy – but I think it was hard for my parents to watch me continuously gain large amounts of weight over the years and push them away when they wanted to help me. I know they were worried for me and perhaps felt a little helpless. They knew I was unhappy, and I was. There is never a

good way to tell someone you love that they need to lose weight. Even if you say it in the nicest, most caring way possible, you probably still can't expect their reaction to be grateful or for them to see it as coming from a 'good' place. I understand that we are all different and we all work differently, so I can only speak from my own experience. As a young child, I overheard comments, and my weight was often pointed out by other children. I knew I looked a little different. But when I was small, my parents would just encourage us to get healthier together as a family and spend more time outdoors doing fun activities.

MAM AND ME AT MY COUSIN'S WEDDING IN SEPTEMBER 2017 – A FEW MONTHS INTO MY JOURNEY.

As I moved into my teenage years, my struggle with my weight became a big part of my everyday life. The worry I carried was crippling. I would open up to my mam about it and was able to talk to her about how I was feeling. This allowed her to listen and understand, and there was no judgement. As I got older, if my mam saw me unhappy, or when I missed out on things, she would know why I was saying no and feeling miserable, even when I wouldn't tell her. But if it was ever brought up to me in a caring way or suggested that this might be the reason why I was feeling the way I was, I would lose my temper so quickly. It would hurt so much that that would be suggested to me. I would shut the conversation down so quickly that my mam would have no choice but to walk away because no matter what she said it would hurt me. I already felt like a failure, so having someone remind me of that was the worst feeling. It made me feel as though they were ashamed of me when they only ever had my best interests at heart. And it would frustrate me because it was all I thought about, and I felt like every day was a losing battle. I spent years of my life going to bed every night, promising myself that tomorrow would be different and I would finally achieve the change I was so desperate for.

But the change didn't happen, and that made me feel like I was letting myself down and letting down those around me too. It affected my moods because it made me so paranoid that, no matter what someone said to me, especially at home, I would think it was a comment about my weight, and I'd harbour all those feelings of frustration and anger inside me all the time. I'm sure some days it was like walking on eggshells around me. But it consumed me; it was all I thought about throughout the day and night. I was obsessed with my size, so when it was mentioned by someone else, it solidified

the idea in my mind that that was all other people thought about me too. I was deeply unhappy, feeling unfit and uncomfortable carrying around the weight, and I had a very unhealthy obsession with my weight that I could never escape. I wanted to lose weight for myself. Not for anyone else.

BUT THE CHANGE DIDN'T HAPPEN, AND THAT MADE ME FEEL LIKE I WAS LETTING MYSELF DOWN AND LETTING DOWN THOSE AROUND ME TOO.

If you have someone in your life who is overweight and you're concerned for them, then that is your own concern. You don't need to project it on to them. I don't think discussing someone's weight or size with them is okay unless they approach you about it first. You may be uncomfortable with their size, but that is your own issue and not theirs. And if they do speak to you about their weight, you can best respond by listening to them without judgement, supporting them in any way you can and letting them know you're always there to chat when they want to. Don't comment on what they have been doing 'wrong' – I am sure they are aware of the changes that need to be made – and don't comment on their food when they're eating it or what they could have instead. I used to get this a lot, and I hated it. But the most important thing to remember is that how we each feel about our own bodies is extremely personal, and for some, it's not an easy thing to talk about. Reassure them of your support and interest if they approach you, but otherwise, don't be surprised if your unsolicited advice is bluntly declined.

//

I FELT THAT I HAD SO MUCH WORK TO DO THAT THERE WAS NO POINT IN PUTTING IN MINIMAL EFFORT OR MAKING SMALL CHANGES.

//

My personal life was another reason that my diet had been taking a hit. I had finally made a small group of close friends at uni and had new friends at work too, and I was trying to find time to socialise with everyone. Like most people in their twenties, I managed to pull it off for a while, getting by on zero sleep and fuelled by sugar-free energy drinks, but it was always at the forefront of my mind just how much my diet and health were taking a back seat. I would think about it all the time while also trying to push it to

the back of my mind. I really wanted to start incorporating healthier foods and options into my life, and I would start and stop all the time. There would always be a reason – some insignificant event coming up – and I would convince myself that there was no point in starting until that was over with. Once that was out of the way, I would realise there was something else happening soon that I wanted to lose weight for, so I would go in all guns blazing until it was too much – and I would throw the towel in.

This was a mistake I made again and again. I would deprive myself of everything and almost punish myself when trying to make healthier changes. I felt that I had so much work to do that there was no point in putting in minimal effort or making small changes. I needed to give it my all so that I could hurry the process up and get to where I wanted to be as quickly as possible.

The first time

One evening, I came home from university and had a couple of hours at home before I was supposed to head back out. This was around the time that I was really struggling to juggle work, uni and my social life with different circles of friends, and nights out were becoming less frequent with my schedule. They usually took place in the student union bar, where you could often only attend if you were a student at the university. I missed out on about 90 per cent of these nights because I didn't live on campus or was working, so on the rare occasion that I could make one, I tried my best.

MY FRIEND DENISE AND ME IN 2012.

Eric and I were basically living together by this point. I had started to worry that he was getting a little jealous that I had my separate life and was a lot busier than he was. I would feel bad that I would be working most weekends and trying to keep up with rehearsals and some social nights. I remember feeling a bit uncomfortable that evening because I knew he was staying in and was trying to convince me to stay in too. I tried to compromise and suggested that I go out for a few hours and come home early. I was meeting my friend before we headed out to celebrate finishing our exams, so I didn't want to bail on her. It turned into an argument, and I told him there was no point in him staying at mine until I got home, and that escalated things. We went

back and forth for a while until he called me a 'fat cow'.

I can still remember the exact feeling I had when I heard the words come out of his mouth. It was like a trigger that brought me back to my childhood and another child shouting a name at me in front of everyone. Eric and I were on our own, but the humiliation felt the same. He hadn't spoken to me like this before, so I had no idea how to respond or even react to what he had said. I was sitting on the end of my bed, and I remember feeling tears coming down my face and trying to pat them away because I didn't want to ruin my make-up. We both just sat there in silence.

I looked at him, waiting for some kind of explanation, but he didn't say anything, so I got up and went to the bathroom. I don't remember feeling angry at all; I was more hurt and embarrassed. Was that what he really thought of me? Once I fixed myself up, I walked back into the bedroom and he apologised, saying he was just frustrated because I was always out. He went home, and I went out to meet my friend. I contemplated telling her what had just happened, but I didn't because I knew the response I would have got – because I knew exactly what I would have said if my friend told me the same thing had happened to her.

I could think of nothing else the entire night. I kept thinking that Eric was doing what I had always feared every other person did: when he looked at me, he only saw my size. Then I started thinking of reasons why he had said it. It was in the heat of the moment because he had been jealous of me having a new social circle. He was trying to get me to stay in with him and did it for a reaction.

Eric had helped me find a new confidence within myself, and I had always felt completely comfortable being myself around him. I had never had that kind of self-confidence before him and had never thought that I would have – but he also had the power to strip me of it.

I told myself it was just a word and that he had apologised for it, that worse things happen and that I could get over this. I had been used to people calling me names my whole life. Sometimes, they did it out of temper, and sometimes, they did it for no reason at all. The names were always related to my weight as it was an easy target, so maybe that was just to be expected from everyone. It didn't necessarily always come from a malicious place, and it was probably just the most obvious way to get at me.

There I was, setting myself up with these low standards for going forward. I was accepting other people's unacceptable behaviours, but why? Probably just to feel accepted. I already had unhealthy boundaries and low self-esteem, so it didn't take much for me to accept or understand why someone might want to speak to me that way. I couldn't tell you the next time Eric called me a name because I don't remember.

I started to feel worse and worse about how I looked. At my lowest, I went to my GP and told them I was desperate. I had paid hundreds of pounds at pharmacies for diet shakes and weight loss products. I had tried juice diets, cabbage

soup diets, every kind of diet, but nothing seemed to work. I had looked into a weight-loss surgery procedure available in the UK, and I thought that was exactly what I needed. The doctor explained that it could be done publicly rather than privately under certain circumstances if I was willing to go on a waiting list. The doctor said that I was a good candidate as I was so young but extremely overweight for my age and height, and the fact that I was relatively healthy helped my chances. I left and told them I would think about it, and I did. I thought about it long and hard and couldn't see many reasons why I wouldn't go for it. I didn't tell anyone at that time because, ten years ago, such surgeries weren't as common as they are today, and I knew my family and friends might encourage a different option because of the risks involved.

I WAS ACCEPTING OTHER PEOPLE'S UNACCEPTABLE BEHAVIOURS, BUT WHY?

But the more I researched it, the more I realised it wasn't for me. There was no guarantee that, after putting myself through a major surgery, I would maintain the weight loss. In fact, I knew there was a strong chance I would be part of the percentage that gained the weight back because I needed to fix my habits first. I had terrible eating habits that were deep and psychologically rooted, and I didn't feel that surgery would fix them for me. I needed to work on my emotional eating, my binge-eating and my secret eating. I knew surgery wouldn't put a stop to that for me in the long term, and so I decided against it. I told myself that it would happen for me when it was supposed to happen.

A brave face

The next few months carried on as normal. Summer rolled around, and I had more time on my hands. I was able to work full-time hours again during the break from university, and Eric and I were enjoying our social life. Our nights out became more frequent, and we also started having a few drinks at home during the week, which wasn't what we normally did.

At this point, Eric was always in and out of new jobs. He would start one for a few weeks and then leave for another, and although it frustrated me, I was being as supportive as I could. From time to time, that meant financially. When he considered changing jobs again, we talked about why he was doing it. Eric had never gone to uni after school, and I suggested that maybe it would be a good idea for him. He attended an open day at a university and decided to apply there; I helped him with all the applications.

I don't think he expected to get accepted to the course, so when he did, it was a big surprise for him. I was just happy that he had something for himself that would keep him focused with a goal in mind.

So, at the end of that summer, we both went to university, me for my second year and him for his first year. In the lead-up to Christmas, we were both busy with our college work, and Eric often asked me to help him with his assignments. Even though I hadn't a clue about his course, I helped him whenever I could. I had my own pile of work to do as well as my job, so it was the last thing I wanted to do most of the time – but I was determined to keep him interested in this course and for him to see it through to the end.

A few days before I was due to fly home to Ireland, I was in my room packing my suitcase. Every Christmas, I went home for at least a week, and I really looked forward to seeing my friends and family. I had all but one piece of uni work finished, so I planned to spend the following two days working on that. I was sitting on the floor beside my case, and Eric and I were talking. He was on his laptop checking his emails when he suddenly began to panic. He had an overdue assignment that he had forgotten all about. I tried to hide my annoyance because I knew what was coming next. I was already telling myself, 'Just say no, you have your own work and that's your priority.'

Straight away, he looked at me and said, 'You have to help me get this in before you go.' I told him straight out what I had told myself: 'No, I have my own work and priorities that I need to finish up before I go.'

I can't remember exactly what was said after that, but I know there was a lot of back and forth and he was really losing his temper with me. I didn't say no often, and he had got used to that, so when I said no to him this time, he got very irritated because I was jeopardising his chances of passing a module. As he got angrier, there was some name-calling, and when he realised that I wasn't budging, he picked up a pile of socks that I had been packing and started throwing them at me as hard as he could. At first, I didn't know whether to laugh or cry because of how silly it seemed, but then I looked at him and saw how serious and angry he was and it didn't seem silly at all anymore.

That was my first experience where he became aggressive and lashed out physically towards me. I put it down to a tantrum because, when he apologised, he kept reiterating that I had no interest in helping him and that's all he was asking for. He had such a sense of entitlement. He couldn't understand that I had my own work to do and that was my main priority. Eventually, I came up with a plan to keep the peace: I would spend the next two days at home with him. We would work side by side and get our stuff done, and when he was stuck, I would help. But he had to do most of it. We got our assignments done and handed in on time and I couldn't have been happier to be leaving London for a week. When I went home, I should have spoken about it to my friends, to perhaps build me up or give me some kind of courage to walk away. But

deep down, I knew I wouldn't have that courage when I came back to London on my own. I had spent all my time with him and had feelings for him, and I was afraid that if I pushed this relationship away, I'd never find one again. I didn't think I'd be lucky enough.

So, like always, I just pushed all my feelings down and locked them away, putting on a brave face. When I returned, I made myself forget what happened, and it seemed like he was good at doing that too.

"

I HAD SPENT ALL MY TIME WITH HIM AND HAD FEELINGS FOR HIM, AND I WAS AFRAID THAT IF I PUSHED THIS RELATIONSHIP AWAY, I'D NEVER FIND ONE AGAIN. I DIDN'T THINK I'D BE LUCKY ENOUGH.

"

Merry-go-round

Over the next few months, things got worse, then they got better, and then worse again. It was a merry-go-round of ups and downs, and I couldn't get off it. Each time things would get worse just by a little, but those times were becoming more frequent. And no matter what went wrong, it always seemed to be my fault. Eric eventually dropped out of university, as he hadn't been showing up enough or putting in the work. This led to a long period of wallowing and angry outbursts. I did have empathy for him because of things he had opened up to me about from his past, but I felt helpless and could do nothing for him, which would guilt me into becoming his support system.

After dropping out of uni, Eric started drinking more than ever. Now we were back to the same cycle of him being in and out of jobs. I was in the second half of my second year at university, and he became more controlling. He wasn't seeing his friends much at all; everyone seemed to be working on themselves or their careers, and I know he was envious of that, and it made him bitter. He would fall out with his friends a lot or talk about them in a bad light to me, as though he was trying to turn me off them too. And he was always texting me when I went to work or to class. I knew he was bored at home and just wanted to talk. But it was constant. If I didn't reply within a certain time, he would get in a huff with me, then ignore me and make me feel bad. It put a horrible pressure on me to always be by my phone, ready to answer and say yes to whatever it was he needed. I don't know why I did, but I still felt sorry for him. I knew he was feeling really lost and didn't know what he wanted to do. I felt like I became the only person he had that he could depend on.

I had so many good people around me at the time, but I was choosing to give most of my energy to Eric. Week by week, things got worse. He became more demanding. He would ask me to skip a rehearsal to come home or to miss catching up with someone so that I'd be home earlier. He'd ask me to pick him things up from the shop when he had been sitting at home all day. He would guilt me when I said no. He would say that I'd be to blame if he walked away for good.

He started to play on my insecurities, too, at first making comments 'in jest' or acting amused in a passive-aggressive way when something positive happened to me. He would lie about things simply to prove a point, but the lie would be so minuscule that it would leave me questioning myself. I then started to think that I was too soft or never looking at things from his point of view. I was constantly second-guessing myself. He knew I was a sensitive person and a people-pleaser, so it didn't take much to make me feel like I was constantly messing up and being the selfish one.

A problem shared

Finally, I opened up to my friend at university about his drinking. She was having boy troubles and I was envious at how comfortable she was at being so open and honest with me. She wasn't embarrassed telling me the not-so-nice things that were happening in her life. But when I tried to open up about my own, I felt so vulnerable – like I would be judged and looked at as stupid. I was already so self-conscious about my physical self; I didn't like to be seen as weak or vulnerable. That day, I wanted to open up to her, so I told her that Eric was drinking a lot more than he should and wasn't listening to me or allowing me to help. I told her I was keeping an eye on it and as soon as I had had enough, I'd be kicking him to the kerb – knowing full well that that was a lie. In fact, I told myself I'd give it a few weeks and then let her know everything was fine again. It felt good to get even a little bit off my chest. His actions were always exaggerated when he'd had alcohol, so a part of me believed that that was the main problem.

I DID EVERYTHING I COULD AS PERFECTLY AS I COULD SO THAT THERE WAS NO ROOM FOR HIM TO COMPLAIN OR NEED TO ASK FOR ANYTHING.

The summer came around, and I was back working full-time, but I wasn't as sociable as I had been the previous summer. It just wasn't worth the trouble with Eric. He had rekindled some old friendships and spent a lot of time with them, and I could go an entire evening without one message from him. When he was out, he didn't feel the need to stay in touch while I was at home, but when he was at home and I was out, it was a different story. He began to get careless when he went out and would come home only to realise that he had lost his bank card, keys, phone or travel pass. This started to happen more and more.

He was never a huge fan of any of my friends and would try to find fault in everything about them. He knew how important my friendships were to me, but he wanted to isolate me. I had been planning to meet a friend for dinner and had already cancelled our two previous dates. As my dinner date got closer, I was anxious about what he might do to ruin it or make me cancel again. But I was determined that I was going this time because, if I was my friend, I would probably have kicked me to the kerb at this stage for all the cancelling and rescheduling.

The restaurant I was going to was only about a 15-minute walk away. My friend and I had said we would do drinks after but hadn't planned where we would go. I knew Eric had lost his travel card a few days before, but he had no plans, so I was hoping he wouldn't ask me for my own travel card. I felt like I was walking on eggshells the day before and the day of the dinner. I did everything I could as perfectly as I could so that there was no room for him to complain or need to ask for anything. I didn't even talk about how much I was looking forward to going out. I made sure not to leave too much time for me to get ready so that he wouldn't get irritated by me getting done up. He didn't look at me or tell me I looked nice when I was ready to go. I tried to act as casually as possible and told him I wouldn't be home late and would give him a text. He asked me what he was supposed to do for the evening and as much as I wanted to say 'I really don't care what you do', I suggested he watch a film or invite a friend over.

Just as I turned to leave, he made a comment about how it wasn't like I cared what he would do because I was just happy to be going out to fill my belly up. I stayed silent and walked out. I didn't want to give him the satisfaction of an argument. When he knew he had no control over me, he would do something or say something rude or condescending to me just as I was leaving because he knew he had the power to ruin my evening. This was one of the things he did that I hated most. It was always so calculated, and it worked every time. When I would go out, I was never relaxed and carefree. I would constantly be checking my phone and my watch. I was never fully present in the moment with the person I was with. Even when I would return home to Ireland for a break, I would have the same feeling in my chest.

That evening I met my friend, and we went for our meal. I tried my best to breathe and just shake it off. I said to myself, *I'm here now, and I can deal with him moping around when I go home.* Our starters hadn't even arrived when I felt my phone vibrate a few times: 'Where are you eating?' 'I want to go out.' 'I'm gonna need your travel card.' They were all sent only minutes apart, but I knew I'd better respond quickly. I had known he was going to ask for my travel card; I had a student card that gave me cheaper fares on transport. I didn't want to give it to him, as he would probably lose it, and I needed it myself to get home. I replied in the most amicable way I could: I told him which restaurant we were in and said that I would need my travel card as I was using it to get home later. I wasn't naïve enough to think he would respond with 'No worries', but I hoped that if I put my phone away and didn't feel it vibrate, maybe I would forget about it.

As we tucked into our meal, I looked up to see Eric looking in at me through the restaurant window. He was calling for me to come outside. My face couldn't hide the look of shock and confusion, mostly as to how he got outside so quickly. He must have already been on the lane looking for me when he sent the texts. I feigned a small chuckle and said, 'Oh my God, look who it is!' to my friend. I grabbed my bag and walked outside without giving her time to respond.

Eric told me straight away that he wasn't impressed that I was ignoring his messages. I could smell the drink off his breath but didn't question him about it. He had no interest in what I had to say – he just wanted the travel card and told me that he was going further out than I was, so I could walk home.

I was conscious that my friend could see us, and I was trying to keep my face as normal-looking as possible. The last thing I wanted was to make some kind of scene. I asked him if he was okay with me walking home on my own late at night, and he told me to just pay the bus fare. I gave him the travel card, walked back in and sat down. It was hard to shake off the feeling. I felt like I needed to burst out crying. He made me feel so powerless. But I kept it together in front of my friend and made up a story about how he was passing by and saw us. I knew she wasn't buying it, but that was my story and I was sticking to it. She said it was odd that he never came in to say hello when he spotted us and instead called me outside. I agreed and blamed his shyness, making excuses for him as usual.

This incident always stayed with me. Even though it wasn't the worst thing he'd done, it was the first time he had done something like it to me in public. I felt as though he was using the environment to his advantage because he knew I wouldn't want to draw any attention to us. It was also the first time someone other than me saw a red flag.

Oh baby, baby

That summer went by quickly. I worked a lot, and Eric and I spent most of our time together in his apartment. He came home drunk to my house on one or two

occasions, and Georgie overheard some of our arguments. She intervened once and said that she could hear him calling me horrible names and speaking to me in a nasty way. I'll never forget how quickly he froze when she entered the room. He was as nice as pie, trying to explain that it was a misunderstanding and that we were both being stupid. Georgie told me to stay with her that night, and I did, but I worried about how upset he would be. I felt humiliated the next day and made excuses, blaming his behaviour on him being drunk. That's why we started spending more time at his place than mine.

Before beginning my final year at university, I went home at the beginning of September for almost two weeks. In the lead-up to going home, I kept thinking that I would just hang on until I went to Ireland and then the two-week break would be a good time for us both to see that maybe we were not right for each other. I was looking forward to having some space and being around my friends and family. I spent a couple of days in Connemara with Aoife, and we had the nicest, most relaxing few days in her family's cottage, walking around the stunning national park and spending cosy evenings by the fire. It was just what I needed. We had spent some holidays there together as little girls and I loved all the stories (mostly ghost stories) she would tell me growing up. I always felt content with Aoife and wanted more than anything to tell her everything that had been going on for the last while, but I just couldn't. I still feared being seen as a disappointment or a failure to the ones who meant the most to me. I knew that once I told her, I could never go back to him. But at that time, it felt as though he was all I had in London. I didn't know if I trusted myself enough to not go back to him.

AOIFE AND ME IN CONNEMARA IN 2015.

Being as close as we were, though, Aoife knew something was up without me saying anything, and when we were out walking one morning, she asked me straight out, 'Are you happy with him?' It caught me off-guard, and I didn't know the answer myself. I told her I wasn't happy with how things were between us but that it could get better. I opened up a little about the drinking and how he could be controlling. I was honest, but not too honest. Just enough so that she knew I wasn't happy with our situation, but not enough for her to think I needed to get away from him.

I felt better after I spoke to Aoife, as though a small weight had been lifted. I hated feeling like I was keeping secrets from my friends. I had created this illusion of my life in London that didn't exist. It made me feel fake and as though I was constantly trying to stay on top of a lie. The plan had been to go shopping for dinner after our walk, but all I remember was waking up about an hour and a half later on the couch. When Aoife went to the bathroom, I had closed my eyes for a minute and was dead to the world, so she did the shopping on her own while I rested. I was not the napping type, so I was surprised that I had managed such a long one.

After our trip, I only had a few days left at home before I headed back to London. I felt much better and was looking forward to starting my final year at uni. I had convinced myself that Eric and I would have a serious conversation about what we were doing before making the decision whether to stay together or not. But I was still afraid to let go of the hope that things could get better if we tried harder and about what I might be throwing away. While I had been in Ireland, we had been in touch every day and hadn't argued, so that made me feel like it might work.

On my final night at home, some of my family dropped in to say goodbye, including my younger cousin Orla. She's six years younger than me, but our mothers are twins, so we've always been very close, despite the age gap. I tried to have a beer with her, but it made me feel sick, so I opted for food instead, as usual. Grazing boards weren't really a thing back then, but I made us something of the sort:

crackers, blueberries, gherkins and cheese. As we picked at it, she joked about the platter looking like a pregnant woman's fantasy. And it did. She made another joke about the beer and said, 'I hope you're not pregnant!'

ME AND ORLA.

I laughed, and it reminded me that Aoife had made a similar joke in Connemara about all my napping. I told myself that I couldn't be; I still didn't get periods and was on the pill. Orla must have seen these thoughts written on my face because she assured me that she was joking. But on the flight home the next day, I couldn't stop thinking about it. I'd been feeling pretty exhausted and some days was nauseated, but I had put that down to worry and stress. I told myself that I was probably being paranoid – I never missed a pill and was pretty convinced I wouldn't be able to get pregnant.

As soon as I landed, I went back to my own house. All I wanted to do was take a pregnancy test, but it was also the last thing I wanted to do. So, on the way home, I decided that I would first unpack, put on a wash and put everything away before heading to the pharmacy. But as soon as I got in the door, I ran into the bathroom, stuck my head in the toilet and threw up. I told myself it was probably the worry I had put on myself, along with not eating and the early flight.

> **I HAD READ THE INSTRUCTIONS SO MANY TIMES THAT I KNEW EXACTLY WHAT THAT MEANT, BUT I REREAD THEM MAYBE SIX OR SEVEN MORE TIMES AFTER THE TEST TO BE SURE.**

I walked to the pharmacy and picked up a few tests. I didn't tell Eric because I was still certain it was a false alarm – I just needed clarification. When I got home, I did the first test and saw the two pink lines. I had read the instructions so many times that I knew exactly what that meant, but I reread them maybe six or seven more times after the test to be sure. I felt numb.

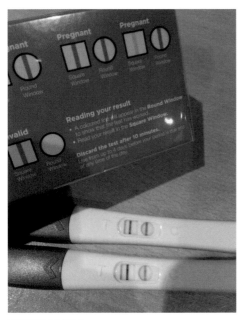

MY PREGNANCY TESTS.

I remember sitting on my bed, and it fell very silent all around. I could hear my heart thumping loudly in my head, and it was all I could focus on. This was not a part of my plan. As you can imagine, a million and one thoughts ran through my mind. I was overwhelmed, scared and emotional. I knew that Eric was coming over in the next hour, so I just sat there and waited until he arrived. I thought he'd know straight away because I felt like it was written all over my face, so I wouldn't need to blurt it out.

But he had no idea. We greeted each other, and he started asking me about my trip and talking normally. I remember that I felt as though I physically couldn't get the words out of my mouth. He was probably there for about 15 minutes before I just came out with it. Understandably, he gave me a funny look and did a thing with his eyebrow that he always did when he was confused. I stood up and took the test from my shelf and showed him. We did the second test together, and it showed the same results.

The next week was a bit of a blur. I told no one but Georgie, and she was a huge support. Eric and I went through every option available to us, and there was a week or two of lots of back-and-forth. I had an early scan near the end of September, and it turned out that I was almost 10 weeks pregnant, which complicated things even further and was also a bigger shock to us both. They told me I was due in April, the same month as my birthday. I was supposed to finish university in May. I had just started back for my final year, and Eric had just dropped out of his course.

I don't remember much of that month because it went by so quickly. I can't even remember going into classes or attending uni that first month back. We both told our families, and they supported us in our decision to go through with it. We decided to move into Eric's apartment permanently. I would leave my house with Georgie after almost seven years of living together. Leaving her was tough because she had no idea how worried I really was, and I wanted to tell her more than anything. I think Eric and I both knew that living together would not be the best thing for us, considering how things had been going before the pregnancy. But ultimately, we decided that we would give it a go and try our best to be all together under one roof.

I made it clear from the start that I would stay in uni for as long as they would allow me to. My course director suggested that I leave before my third trimester and return the following September once the baby was born. I was just so relieved to have a plan in place and know that I would still be able to finish my degree. At the time, when I explained this plan to everyone, I could see the look of doubt on their faces. I had no idea what raising a newborn would be like, but everyone seemed certain that I would not be able to manage both. Eric used to laugh at me and remind me it was only a drama degree; it wasn't the end of the world if I didn't get it.

Downhill from here

The move from my house to Eric's was quick, maybe about two weeks after we decided. It made sense as his family home was across the road, and I knew that I would need plenty of support. Those two weeks before the move were not good: tensions were high, and we were both scared and unprepared. His way of coping was to drink more.

I organised a man with a van to take my stuff over on moving day. I had gathered quite a collection of furniture in the previous seven years. My bedroom was on the third floor of a three-storey,

Victorian-style house, so I knew it would be a job-and-a-half getting some of the bigger furniture down. The man with the van was coming at midday and had informed me that he didn't do most of the lifting; he would just pack the van. Eric was going out the night before the move, and I was delighted because I could give my room one final deep clean before leaving and enjoy my last night with Georgie. But he assured me that he would be there the next day to pack up the van. Of course, the next day came and he was nowhere to be seen. As it got closer and closer to the time that the moving van was arriving, I became more and more stressed. I knew that he would have had one too many and was still sleeping. At the time, I had no car, so I couldn't drive over to him. All I could do was keep ringing his phone in the hope that he'd wake up.

The man with a van arrived and was highly unimpressed to be a man down and left with a pregnant lady and a roomful of boxes and furniture up two flights of stairs. I was on my own in the house, but I tried my best to get as much down as possible. I carried most of the boxes and suitcases downstairs for him. When we got to the final pieces of furniture, where two people were definitely needed, he told me that we would have to leave them for another day as he couldn't manage them alone, and I agreed. As frustrated as I was, he was right.

I tried one last time to call Eric, as I was now starting to panic about arriving at his house to unload everything while he was sleeping. To my surprise, he answered and said that he was five minutes away –

so we'd be able to move the furniture after all. Eric didn't sound very chirpy, though. When he arrived, he stank so strongly of alcohol that I was convinced he had got drunk that morning. If I could smell it so clearly off him, then so could the man, and I was mortified. The last part took longer than we had thought because getting large furniture down angled, narrow staircases in London houses is not an easy job. Every time Eric went back up to get another item, he would almost scowl at me, and I would pretend to be unaware of how annoyed he was growing. The sweat was pumping out of him and I knew it was the alcohol. When we finally got to Eric's place, the man with the van told me to go in and make myself a cup of tea and that they would grab everything.

THE MAN WITH A VAN ARRIVED AND WAS HIGHLY UNIMPRESSED TO BE A MAN DOWN AND LEFT WITH A PREGNANT LADY AND A ROOMFUL OF BOXES AND FURNITURE UP TWO FLIGHTS OF STAIRS.

I was dreading the removal man leaving, as unbeknown to him, he was keeping the peace. As soon as he left, the atmosphere changed. Eric started shouting at me about the amount of stuff I had, how we would never fit everything in, and how I could have helped more instead of watching. He was getting worked up, and the sweat was still dripping off him. I asked if he had drunk anything already today. He started screaming at me for turning it on him, that it was my things all over the place that were annoying him and that I needed to get them all put away today. I told him that I would be unpacking but I wasn't going to have everything done on the same day.

Before I even finished my sentence, Eric shoved me hard into my small toiletries trolley. I fell over and knocked the trolley with me. I used my hands to break my fall and, luckily, I wasn't hurt – just shocked. Hundreds of cotton earbuds covered the floor.

Eric had walked away as soon as he pushed me. Seconds later, when he re-entered the room, I was expecting the usual apology. But instead, I had a dustpan and brush thrown at me and was told to clean up the mess I had made. He left the house. I just sat in silence for a long time. I don't think I even cried for the first while. I remember thinking that this was going to be my life now and it wasn't going to get better. A part of me knew that I was only accepting this because I didn't expect any better for myself. Eric had done things to me before with aggression, but never this kind of physical aggression. A day that should be an exciting time for most people had turned out to be one of the worst days I'd ever had. As soon as I gave up my freedom and my safe space to move into his place, this happened.

||

BEING OVERWEIGHT IS HARD, BUT BEING OVERWEIGHT AND PREGNANT IS REALLY HARD.

||

The next few months were even harder as I became more and more isolated. I was working three jobs, and my friends were all busy. I never socialised anymore and just spent my time between work, home and Eric's parents' house. As the pregnancy went on, he started drinking more. Most days, he would drink at any time of the day. He began drinking different spirits, and whatever was in them made him behave differently – either that or he was drinking a lot more. He was not a nice person.

He could go a few days without drinking, and we would get on and have some normality. It was such a relief to not be walking on eggshells. We would have serious conversations about him getting help. He would get emotional and tell me that he didn't want to be like this when the baby arrived. I knew that he was deeply unhappy and hated how he was behaving. Still, I also had my rose-tinted

glasses on and forgot that the abuse was a choice that he was making. I didn't understand at the time that, no matter what I did or how hard I tried, I would never be able to help him or make him sort himself out. That was an inside job. But I wanted to be there and support him so that I wouldn't be harming our baby's chance of ever having a family.

I had decided I would work until two weeks before my due date. Being overweight is hard, but being overweight and pregnant is really hard. I hated the fact that it wasn't obvious that I was pregnant. The doctors at the hospital would remind me at every appointment that I was overweight, which was a higher risk for my pregnancy. They even asked me to be part of a clinical trial for obese pregnant women, which was looking at the connection between gestational diabetes and obesity. I never got gestational diabetes while pregnant. I didn't gain much weight at all, even though I was growing a baby inside me. I think the doctors were just happy I wasn't putting extra weight on. My lack of appetite was linked to my stress at home, but I was also conscious of what I was putting into my body while I was pregnant. I had never treated my body with much respect concerning what I put into it until I became pregnant. It changed things for me. I wasn't just feeding myself; I was feeding my little baby too, and I wanted him or her to be as healthy as possible. I wanted to do whatever I could to make sure they were thriving inside me.

But Eric had started to get physical with me more regularly. I was able to hide it well because I was so isolated, and he never really marked my face during this time. The physical abuse was not only dangerous to the baby but to me too, and yet I was still too afraid to leave. I had nowhere to go, and I was heavily pregnant. Who wanted that turning up on their doorstep? I can't explain how I felt; all I know is that I felt stuck. I didn't want to tell his family or my friends in London because of the shame and the fear of what he would do if he knew I had told people.

The verbal and emotional abuse was the hardest for me. I worried about how the stress a mother feels can be passed on to their baby. But I couldn't control my stress. Eric told me every day that it was my fault and I was probably stressing the baby out because of how much I cried and worried. He started to speak to me in a demeaning way most days. Listening to that, when I already struggled with my own inner voice and confidence, made the voices in my head that bit louder. I began to believe them more and more because I was hearing it from the outside too. The voices were taking over, and with every day that passed I became a little more worthless to myself. The guilt I felt inside is something that I still struggle with. I know what most people would think: I was selfish to stay around and put myself in that dangerous situation while I was pregnant. It made me feel like the worst mam in the world before I even got to meet my baby. But it wasn't that black and white to me. There were so many emotions and fears attached to my reasons for staying.

The talk

One day, Eric's family members called me at work to say that they had picked him up on the street, drunk, in the middle of the day. We decided that we would all have a serious sit-down and that I should go to their house straight away after work. I felt such a sense of relief. Maybe hearing from his family that he had an issue with alcohol, and knowing that he had all of our support, was just what he needed.

THE VOICES WERE TAKING OVER, AND WITH EVERY DAY THAT PASSED I BECAME A LITTLE MORE WORTHLESS TO MYSELF.

When I arrived, the atmosphere was calm. We all sat together and spoke about the situation and what we could do that would help him. I told them how bad it had been lately and that he had been dropped home by the police on more than one occasion for being intoxicated, with zero recollection of it the next day. He was spending and losing his money constantly and not helping me financially. I opened up about his angry outbursts, like the time he got so frustrated with me that he threw my perfume bottles out the window onto the road. But I didn't tell them that he was physical with me, although I don't think it would have shocked them. I expressed my fears about going into labour at any time and him not being contactable – that was a big worry of mine then. When we left, he wasn't angry or upset with me; he just seemed relieved, as though all along it had been a cry for help and he was happy now that he was being heard.

In the last couple of weeks of my pregnancy, there were no incidents; Eric made a big effort to stop drinking, and we stayed in most evenings. I was pleased to not have that constant worry when he was out drinking, but I also felt as though I was sitting on a time bomb. I wasn't naive enough to think that he would change overnight and that there would be no more incidents. I was still riddled with anxiety, tiptoeing around him to make sure that he was okay and doing everything I could to keep the peace.

New beginnings

My contractions started around midnight on Friday, 8 May 2015. I was almost two weeks overdue, but at last, my baby was ready to come out and meet his mammy. I stayed as calm as I could, and Eric ran

me a bath to try to ease the discomfort. It was after 3 o'clock in the morning when I knew it was time to go to the hospital. Luckily, labour didn't last long. During it, the baby decided to pass some meconium (just like their own mammy did!), and I was pulled down for an emergency C-section.

At 8.25 a.m., my boy Carter was handed to me. I felt a rush of emotions that I had never felt before. It was overwhelming, like fireworks going off inside me while I tried to remain present and take it all in. They took him away to be weighed and checked, and I was left to be stitched up for what felt like the longest time in the world. I lay there crying because I couldn't remember what he looked like, and I had only seen him ten minutes before. I was probably a little high on life ... and pain medication!

U

AT 8.25 A.M., MY BOY CARTER WAS HANDED TO ME.

U

By lunchtime, we were back in our room, and I was just staring at every perfect inch of him. It was a Friday morning, and I knew I wouldn't be home until late afternoon on Sunday. My parents were back in Ireland, and Eric's parents were on holiday, so his big sister was a huge help. It was the happiest I had seen Eric in such a long time, and I couldn't help but feel emotional. But my bubble quickly burst. His sister suggested that he get me a nice lunch instead of having to eat the hospital food, and I got a sick feeling in my tummy. I just knew that he was on cloud nine and would want to celebrate with his friends – and a drink.

He left at around one o'clock and came back after nine o'clock that evening with no nice lunch but full of booze. He was the sloppy kind of drunk. It's hard to have a private conversation with a drunk person when you're in a room of six other beds and five other families, with only curtains between you all. He didn't care that other people could hear, and I was so drained and focused on the baby that I didn't have the energy to argue back. I didn't want to cause a scene, so when he asked me to sit in the chair so that he could lie in the bed, I did. And when he called me the most disgusting names and reminded me that nobody would ever go near me if I left him, I said nothing. I had nothing to give him. When he left, the man in the cubicle beside me checked on me, and I just smiled at him. I didn't need to say anything, I was humiliated enough. The next day, that man's wife came in to see Carter and asked me all about him and let me indulge. She gave me loads of magazines and a bag of sweets as she was being discharged that day. She didn't mention anything about the night before or what she had heard, but her kindness always stayed with me.

I told Eric's sister that he had been drunk the night before and that I didn't want him to show up like that again. He had a wristband that allowed him entry 24/7, so she spoke to security and explained the situation. They said they would refuse him entry if he turned up with drink on him. That gave me peace of mind for 24 hours. He did, of course, show up drunk the next evening, and when he rang me to tell me they wouldn't let him in, I faked disbelief and said that I would try to talk to security. My time in the hospital is not a very pleasant memory, but I had hours and hours of bonding time with Carter on my own that I will cherish forever.

CARTER AND ME A FEW HOURS AFTER HE WAS BORN. IT'S THE ONLY PICTURE I HAVE OF HIM AS A NEWBORN.

On Sunday evening, I was discharged, and Eric was there, sober. I got us a taxi home, only to discover that he had locked his keys in the house along with mine. I called a locksmith to come and save the day and charge me double as it was an out-of-hours call. I didn't even speak to Eric that evening, although he was trying hard to be nicer than usual, which made me more irritated.

Don't go

The next few weeks were the hardest of my life. I was coming to terms with being a new mam while also recovering from major surgery. Day-to-day errands were already a struggle for me, at over 20 stone, but now everything seemed hard, especially with a newborn in my arms. The day after we left the hospital, there was no food in the house, so I popped Carter into the buggy and walked over to the supermarket. I bumped into Eric's brother, who was disgusted that I was up and walking around, never mind doing grocery shopping. I laughed and said that I felt fine and that the shop was only five minutes away. I just wanted some bits in for when my parents arrived. They were coming to visit the next day for a week and would stay in a hotel around the corner.

Eric tried to be on his best behaviour while they were there. On two occasions, however, he came home tipsy in the evening. I made a joke about him being out wetting the baby's head with friends. He wasn't working at this point, but I lied to everyone and told them he was so that they wouldn't be worried. When my parents would leave our house in the evenings, he would take it out on me, saying that he felt uncomfortable in his own home and that I was being rude and disrespectful to him. That week was a nightmare, with me trying to keep everything under control so as not to worry anyone. I was emotional but also numb and physically drained.

ME AND CARTER.

On the day my parents were leaving, they had a mid-morning flight, so I knew that they would call over for one last quick cuddle before their taxi collected them. I didn't want them to leave. I felt safe when they visited because Eric was always afraid to do things to me when other people were there. The night before, Eric went out, and I had put myself and Carter to bed early. At about 5 o'clock that morning, he arrived home, and it was probably the most intoxicated I had ever seen him. He couldn't speak properly, and his words made no sense. He was almost bouncing off the walls. *Oh, Jesus,* I thought. *I have less than four hours to sober him up.* I got up as quickly as I could. I still had all my stitches, so moving quickly was painful and dangerous. He was the kind of drunk where he just wanted to fight. If I was nice, it would annoy him. If I was annoyed, it would aggravate him, and if I ignored him, it would irritate him. It was a lose-lose situation, so I spent the next few hours going with it.

He wanted to hold the baby, but I said that he had just fallen asleep, so we should go into the other room and cook Eric something to line his stomach. But he had no interest. He started shouting rubbish about me wanting to take his baby away from him one day, and I begged him to keep his voice down. I was so scared that he would wake Carter.

When Eric moved into the bedroom where Carter was sleeping, I followed him. There was no way he was in a state to pick up a baby. He said he wanted to take him for a walk, and I told him that that was ridiculous. It was the very early hours of the morning, and raining. But he just didn't like that I was saying no. I stood in front of the Moses basket and blocked him from getting closer, but he pushed me onto the bed. I got straight back up, and he hit me the hardest he had ever hit me, on the side of my face. I thought the room was going slanty, but I was falling to the floor.

I was probably only out for a few seconds, but when I opened my eyes, Eric looked worried. As soon as he saw me get up, he relaxed a bit and stormed out of the room. It was bright at this point, and I knew my mam and dad would be arriving soon. I sat down to try to figure out what I would do. My head was throbbing and felt like it was twice the size it should be. I needed to calm Eric down, sober him up and hopefully get him to sleep before my parents arrived. I made him food and put him in the bedroom on his own. I talked calmly to him, and by the time he finished his food, he was out for the count. I got Carter fed and dressed and then checked my face in the mirror. It was really red, so I needed to put some make-up on. I looked in the mirror and took the biggest breath. *Just don't cry*, I told myself. *This is definitely the final straw, and once my parents leave, I will find a way out of this situation for Carter and for me.*

When my parents arrived, I told them that Eric was having a nap as he was on the night feeds and only managed to get to sleep at about 6 o'clock. When they were going, they wanted to say goodbye to him, so I went in to wake him, with no idea how he would react. Thankfully, he got up and managed to pull himself together and go out and say goodbye. When my mam hugged me and told me she was proud of me, I lost it. The tears started and they wouldn't stop. I took her hand and said, 'Mam, please don't leave me. I don't want you to go.' That set her off, but my dad reassured me that I was doing a great job and that they would be back in a few weeks. He shook Eric's hand and told him to look after me. They left, and my first week of being a mam was over.

Eric talked to me like normal, like nothing had happened five hours earlier. Later, he asked me what had happened to my face. It had been the worst night of my life, and he couldn't even remember it. He just woke up the next day with zero recollection of what he had done to me and what he put me through. He would never understand what I had to witness because he had the pleasure of blacking out. I had gone through hell, and he didn't even remember.

The mark

A few days later, Eric's brother called over unannounced to see how we were getting on. I was sitting on the floor, playing with Carter, and when I glanced up at him, he gave me a funny look. He walked over to me and lifted my chin up towards the light.

'What's that on your face?' he asked.

I was lost for words.

He looked at his brother and back at me and said, 'Jen, the side of your face is black and blue.'

I WAS TIRED OF HIDING AND MAKING UP LIES AND STORIES ABOUT HOW CLUMSY I WAS.

I got up and walked to the bathroom mirror to buy some time to think of what I would say. His brother told me to wipe away my make-up, and I did. I couldn't deny that my right temple and eye socket down to my jaw were badly bruised. They both stood there, looking at me, and I just burst out crying. I was tired of hiding and making up lies and stories about how clumsy I was. His brother turned to Eric and asked him if he had done it. Eric just kept his focus on me; he told me to tell his brother what had happened to me. So, I did.

I TOLD MY MAM THAT I HAD GOT MYSELF A STUDIO FLAT TEMPORARILY. SHE HAD NO IDEA IT WAS A WOMEN'S SHELTER.

Eric's brother told him how disgusted he was and said that it wouldn't happen again. He started to pack up Carter's things and told me to fill a case because we were leaving now and would be staying with him in Eric's family house. Panic set in for me now, too. Had I made a mistake? I had a 10-day-old baby and minutes to pack up our life. I couldn't see through my tears and I couldn't think. But I grabbed the essentials and we left. Eric begged us not to go, saying that it wouldn't happen again and that he didn't want me to take Carter away. At that moment, I felt sorry for him.

Eric's brother called his sister that night to tell her everything. She was upset. She had me move in with her family and her for a week while we figured things out. It was awful. I was so grateful, but I also felt incredibly uncomfortable and in the way. All I wanted was to be in my own home, surrounded by my own things.

When Carter was just over a month old, I moved into a women's shelter. It was a small studio flat with a kitchenette and a separate shower and toilet. While I was living there, Eric went to rehab and gave up the drink. His family was the biggest support to me. I didn't tell my family or friends what I was going through. I was mortified and didn't want to cause any upset. I told my parents that we were on a break and that he was drinking a little too much, so he was going to focus on himself and get better. I told my mam that I had got myself a studio flat temporarily. She had no idea it was a women's shelter.

I would wake up every day and look at the same four walls. Nobody knew where I was, and the shelter was in an area that I wasn't familiar with. Most days I would carry Carter's pram down two flights of stairs and walk up and down the high street. I would buy myself crap food every day as it was one of my only small pleasures. I didn't have a television, so I watched my laptop all day. Carter was still at the age where he slept a lot. It was very lonely.

Just before I returned to university, I moved into a two-bedroom apartment in Croydon, where the rent was much cheaper. Eric's mam would look after Carter while I went back to study. I got myself a little car to make getting around easier, as we now lived far out. Eric and I were still in contact, and I knew he was off the drink and nearing the end of rehab and starting a new job. He got to see Carter when we were at his mam's house. The weeks went by, and there were no incidents. We were talking more and seeing each other more. I was finding my feet again at uni, and although it was tough because I didn't know anyone, as all my friends had graduated before me and moved on, I kept to myself this time. I had zero interest in socialising or making friends;

I just wanted to get this degree over with.

Over the next few months, Eric, Carter and I spent more and more time together as a family and at my new apartment. Things felt better than they had been before, and, I hate to admit it, I was happy that the three of us could enjoy time together and make memories. We spent Carter's first Christmas with Eric's family, and I allowed myself to look forward to the new year.

ME AND CARTER.

The last time

Just before Christmas, Eric had started a new job where the money was better. But as soon as he got paid, everything turned upside down.

The following seven months were a rollercoaster of abuse. It was worse than before. The punches were harder, the beatings were longer, and the mental torture pushed me over the edge. I would ask myself every minute of the day, *Why am I still staying?* I still can't answer that. Feeling so helpless and worthless is a pain I can't describe. It was unbearable, and every single day I would question my sanity. I felt completely powerless.

There were so many incidents that should have been the final one. I had dirty nappies thrown in my face, my debit cards were stolen, I was locked outside my apartment at three o'clock in the morning, I had chairs broken on my back, his hands around my throat, my uni laptop was pawned, my house keys were taken off me for days at a time, my car keys were taken off me so I couldn't make it to an exam, hair brushes were thrown at me that cut my head open, I was left sleeping on the floor for nights with no blankets or pillows, given the silent treatment for days, had neighbours calling the police on multiple occasions because of what they could hear. Not once did I press charges. I had things done to me that I will never be able to talk about. I was broken. I was living a life that no one had any idea I was living.

We didn't live together for those seven months, but Eric showed up when he felt like it. His parents tried as much as they could to talk to him, and he would reset for a week. He lost his job for turning up intoxicated. When planning to finally leave, I always said, 'I'll just get this assignment out of the way first,' or, as time passed, 'I'll just wait until after Carter's birthday,' or 'I'll just wait until I graduate.' There was always something.

In May, I only had one month left at university and had to submit a 12,000-word thesis. To this day, I have no idea how I wrote it. But I was so determined to prove myself and everyone else wrong. I wanted to do this for Carter and for myself. I handed everything in and got my degree with a higher grade than I had expected. I was so proud. But by the time I graduated, I felt nothing but hatred for Eric.

My parents flew over to celebrate with me and be the support they didn't know I needed.

MY DAD AND ME ON MY GRADUATION.

One afternoon, I heard Eric stumble up the driveway. I didn't want to deal with him, and Carter was awake. Eric was too drunk to engage in any kind of conversation, but whatever I said, he didn't like it. He put Carter in his cot and came back to me. He was never physically violent towards me when Carter was in the same room, so I knew what was coming. He lit a cigarette in the sitting room; I told him to go outside but he ignored me. The cigarette ash was falling everywhere, and I just had to bite my tongue. As soon as he finished it, I heard Carter calling for me, so I went to get him. I picked him up and held him in my arms.

Eric asked me to drop him off on the high street near his house. It was a long drive from my apartment and I didn't want to be in the car with him, so I told him that I would another day. He lit another cigarette, and I told him to get out of the house. He ran towards me while Carter was still in my arms and grabbed me by the throat. I was in shock, but I tried my best not to react or frighten Carter. Eric took his cigarette from his mouth and held it to my cheek, threatening to burn me if I didn't drive him.

"

I KNEW THAT I WAS PUTTING CARTER IN DANGER JUST AS MUCH AS ERIC WAS.

"

That was my moment. I knew that I was putting Carter in danger just as much as Eric was. He had never been violent to me in front of our son, so I had naively thought that no harm could come to Carter. I stayed as calm as possible and agreed to drop him off. I strapped Carter into his car seat, and we got in the car. I

stopped at a red light, and Eric started shouting at me. Silent tears streamed down my face because this was one of the scariest situations I had ever been in with him. He had his keys in his hand and kept poking me in the face with them. I stared straight into the car in front, where a man was staring back at me in the rear-view mirror. All I could think was, *Please get out of your car and help me.* But he didn't. We arrived, and as soon as Eric stepped out of the car, I promised myself, *That's it; this is going to be the last incident I ever have with him.* He got out, closed the door, and I drove away.

Telling someone

I ended up at a Burger King drive-through and ordered some chips for Carter. Then I parked in an IKEA car park and cried. I felt like a terrible mother for feeding my 15-month-old baby chips in the back of a car, but he was loving life. I was too afraid to go home because Eric would show up there.

This was the moment I made an important decision. I told myself to text a friend to tell them. *Just send the text*, I kept telling myself. *Once you send it, it's done.* My hands were shaking, but I sent the message, and of course she told me to collect her from work and that she would stay the night. I told her everything.

I can't tell you how scary it was to open up to someone so much, but also how good it felt to get it all off my chest. She listened to everything I had to say and didn't judge me or push me to say more than I wanted. I think maybe she knew, deep down, that things hadn't been right with me for a long time.

CARTER AT ABOUT 7 WEEKS OLD, WHEN WE WERE LIVING IN A SHELTER.

Around 6 o'clock in the morning, I heard footsteps coming down the driveway. I sat up and woke my friend. I heard Eric whistle, and then a stone hit the window. Mr friend told me to stay there, and she went to the window. It was bright out, so she could immediately see the state he was in. She told him to go home and that he was too drunk to come in to see Carter, which infuriated him. She let him know that if he didn't leave now, she would call the police. There was a skip in the garden with an old wardrobe in it. He took some bits of the broken wardrobe and, even though I was on the second

floor, he managed to smash the windows in my sitting room and bedroom as he was in such a rage. He then went on to smash my car windows before walking away. I sat on the edge of the bed in complete panic while my friend handled the situation by phoning the police. Carter didn't wake once.

When the police arrived, I told them what had happened, and three officers in an unmarked car stayed with us for a few hours because I knew he would return. He was calling and texting me non-stop, and one of the police officers asked if she could listen to the voicemail in another room. I had no idea what he was going to be saying in them. I was humiliated. In the early afternoon, he showed up again and was arrested.

"

JUST SEND THE TEXT, I KEPT TELLING MYSELF. ONCE YOU SEND IT, IT'S DONE.

"

The scare

Eric and I never had contact again after that day. The year that followed was a long year of restraining orders, court dates, living in fear and being unable to leave the country. He showed up drunk outside my house late one night on my birthday the following April, but he didn't see me from my window, and I called the police straight away. The only times after that I saw him were the court dates he attended regarding my decision to move Carter and myself home to Ireland. We mostly avoided eye contact, but his presence alone still had a powerful hold on me. I wanted to walk into the courtroom with my head held high and feel empowered, but I didn't. As soon as I saw him, I felt two feet tall. These cases can go on for a long time, and there's always a lot of back and forth between each party. Every time I thought we were nearing the end, a further date would be set in another six weeks.

HE SHOWED UP DRUNK OUTSIDE MY HOUSE LATE ONE NIGHT ON MY BIRTHDAY THE FOLLOWING APRIL, BUT HE DIDN'T SEE ME FROM MY WINDOW, AND I CALLED THE POLICE STRAIGHT AWAY.

Going through the most private, vulnerable things and sharing photographs of my injuries and videos of his verbal abuse to a roomful of strangers was exhausting and demeaning. The whole experience made me more anxious than I had ever been before. I was always looking over my shoulder. I never wanted to be anywhere quiet, where there weren't many people around. Even when walking through the garden to my car, I was always waiting for him to appear. His family were disappointed and hurt that I wanted to move back home, and they stopped staying in touch with us too. For a while that year, Carter and I were isolated from everyone.

Before Christmas, I had a scare where I was taken by ambulance to A&E because I thought I was having a heart attack, but it turned out to be acute pancreatitis and gastritis. I had to spend two nights in hospital. I was lucky that I had a friend, who Carter adored, looking after him. I needed surgery, but it couldn't be performed in that hospital because my BMI was too high, so I was referred to another hospital. I never followed this up, but thankfully, I never experienced the pain again. I'm sure it was my body's way of reacting to all my stress and the extra weight I had rapidly gained that year. But this health scare was a real eye-opener for me. It was my first time in a scary medical situation that was due to my weight. What if something worse had happened? What about Carter? Where would he go? He didn't deserve that. He had only one parent raising him now, and he deserved the healthiest version I could be.

IT WAS MY FIRST TIME IN A SCARY MEDICAL SITUATION THAT WAS DUE TO MY WEIGHT.

The plan

I started trying my best to eat three proper meals. I cooked the best foods for Carter and gave him three great meals a day so that I could do the same for myself. I bought myself a scale, because it had been years since I weighed myself. The last time had probably been in the hospital during pregnancy, and I usually closed my eyes. I knew that in the year after Carter was born, I had gained a substantial amount of weight in a very short time. That period was when my emotional eating was at its worst. I didn't leave the house much, and in the evenings, after I put Carter to bed, I would sit and eat my feelings. My choices had been to either sit with my thoughts and cry or distract myself with bags of crisps, chocolates and ice cream.

I stepped on the scales, and, to my horror, they couldn't tell my weight because they only went up to 25 stone. I was heartbroken. I hadn't thought I was 25 stone, let alone more than that. It took a

while before I was brave enough to buy a new scale. After a month of eating more healthily, I felt better in myself but didn't feel like any weight had come off me. I had assumed that, at my size, the weight would fall off if I changed my diet drastically. I went to see my GP for some advice. My mam had recently been diagnosed with Graves' disease, and her doctor had said it could be hereditary on the maternal side. When I told the doctor this, he did my bloods. It turned out I did have a very underactive thyroid, so I began taking medication for it. He explained that the medication could take a couple of months to work. I tried my best to stay as healthy as possible during that time, and my meals were definitely better. However, I was still bingeing in the evenings.

I STEPPED ON THE SCALES, AND, TO MY HORROR, THEY COULDN'T TELL MY WEIGHT BECAUSE THEY ONLY WENT UP TO 25 STONE.

Not long into the new year, my solicitor told me that I would probably get the go ahead to move home around late spring. I couldn't believe it was finally happening. I told myself that I wouldn't get excited until I was actually leaving the country. But soon, the excitement simmered down a little and was replaced with dread. I didn't want to move home in the state I was in. I always said I felt like a failure, but this was me at my lowest. I was a single parent, moving back in with my mam and dad, aged 28 and weighing over 25 stone, with no job and no plan. I wanted to be proud of the job I was doing with Carter on my own, but all I could think of was how much I would be judged. I shouldn't have cared about any of that because I knew that all my family and friends just wanted me home safe. But it was all I thought about. I was terrified of anyone thinking I was a failure to Carter.

Around this time, the summer of 2017, Carter turned two years old. He was the wildest little firecracker of a boy I had ever met and was getting to the stage of never wanting to be in his buggy. I needed to be able to keep up with him. He had my energy and was so confident and sociable. For the first time in a long time, it looked like things were going to start getting better for us, and I could feel my old self coming back a little bit more every day. I felt excited when I got up in the morning. That feeling of Groundhog Day gradually left me, and I felt motivated to make more positive changes while things were good. I looked into joining a slimming group because I knew my friend Grace had had good success with one, but I was too self-conscious to go to the meeting. I reached out and asked her for help. Grace couldn't have done more. She explained the basics to me and told me to send her pictures of all of my meals so

that she could explain to me what I needed to adapt. I bought myself a fancy food diary, and one day I sat on the floor with Carter to fill it in. While he coloured in pictures, I planned.

CARTER AND ME IN 2017.

I wrote lists of foods I was allowed to have, organised my meals and wrote a shopping list. I stuck these pages all over my kitchen presses so that my plan was as simplified and accessible to me as possible. I bought a new scale that went up to 33 stone and finally got a reading of my weight. I was almost 26 stone. I know I had been heavier before I started trying to eat more healthily, but this was the heaviest weight I had ever recorded. I didn't let it get to me, though, and every time I had thoughts like, *I need to lose 10 stone! It will take forever!*, I would stop myself and say, 'I can only focus on today and what I can do today, so I am not worrying about the future.'

The food diary I bought was a 12-week planner that was pink and, on the cover, read 'Happy Girls Are The Prettiest'. I made a promise to myself that I would complete it, and even if there were days that I didn't stick to what I had planned, I would still stay accountable to myself. It was 12 weeks of work, but I told myself that this would surely be achievable, considering I had got through the previous three years. I dated my first entry 1 June 2017, and every week on a Thursday I would weigh myself. I planned my days so that I wasn't depriving myself or leaving myself feeling hungry. I usually enjoyed a sweet treat when Carter was asleep in the evenings, so I made sure to include that every day in the beginning. I would think of meals I enjoyed and then adapt them to work for me by doing simple things like making my sauces from scratch, cooking with less oil, baking rather than frying and breading my own chicken and fish rather than using store-bought. There are so many small changes you can make when cooking that make a big difference towards making your meals healthier. I looked on social media a lot for meal inspiration and help. I didn't focus too much on exercise, but I tried my best to leave the house with Carter more for some fresh air and playtime. Some days I couldn't, but when I could, I did.

After three weeks, I was down almost 17 pounds. I couldn't believe it. Why was it working this time? How was I still enjoying it? The fear always lingered in the back of my mind: that that feeling would soon fade away and I would be back to square one. But I tried my best to remain positive and trust my gut that this was my time and Carter was pushing me to finally do it.

Listening to your gut is a phrase I often hear, but I struggled with it for a long time. It's hard to trust your gut when, because of all the deep-rooted feelings of failure, your gut is usually telling you something won't work. I would think, *What's the point? I am just going to mess it up anyway.* But this time it felt a little different.

A FEW MONTHS INTO MY JOURNEY, WHEN I WAS DOWN A FEW STONE. I TOOK THESE PROGRESS PICTURES EVERY 6 TO 8 WEEKS FOR MYSELF.

IT'S HARD TO TRUST YOUR GUT WHEN, BECAUSE OF ALL THE DEEP-ROOTED FEELINGS OF FAILURE, YOUR GUT IS USUALLY TELLING YOU SOMETHING WON'T WORK.

Week Three was a big week because it was our final hearing in court, and I was told that Carter and I were granted leave from the UK for permanent residency in Ireland. A day that I thought would never come had finally arrived. I rang my parents, and within 30 minutes, my dad had a van and ferry organised for a few days later and was going to come to collect us both. The weather that week in London was scorching hot and not the ideal weather for packing up a house on my own with a toddler in less than three days. But we did it. My dad arrived on the evening of 20 June after driving from the ferry in Wales. We got a takeaway to celebrate and spent the next day packing the van, and then we left together in the early hours of 22 June.

CARTER AND ME IN TYMON PARK, TALLAGHT, SOON AFTER WE MOVED HOME IN THE SUMMER OF 2017.

I was already conscious about the amount of food I would be surrounded by when I arrived back home, with all the gatherings and nights out, but I just reminded myself of how consistent I had been and how good I'd been feeling. I wasn't going to let anything stop me.

Home

WALKING INTO MY PARENTS' HOUSE THAT FIRST DAY, IT WAS LIKE ALL THE WEIGHT I WANTED TO LOSE WAS LIFTED OFF ME.

The experience of arriving home is hard to put into words. The shame lifted as soon as I was surrounded by family and friends. I felt supported and loved. Walking into my parents' house that first day, it was like all the weight I wanted to lose was lifted off me. That constant, heavy feeling of everything piling up on me immediately lightened. However, I knew I had a long road of recovery ahead of me and just being back home wasn't enough to fix my problems. Even though I was grateful to be home, I wasn't happy within myself. Nothing material or external would change that: no amount of money, nights out, new jobs, new relationships. Happiness comes from within, and I needed to work on myself from the inside out. I needed to learn to be completely happy on my own and not to rely on anyone or expect anyone else to give that to me.

CARTER AND MY PARENTS.

And so began the era in which I was ready to completely and wholeheartedly focus on myself and my happiness. Only in doing so could I truly become the best version of myself for Carter. For the first time, I didn't feel guilty taking time away from Carter and putting my needs higher up on my list of priorities. This did not mean being less present than I had been. It was about finding that healthy balance that worked for us both so I could be a better parent physically and mentally.

The first few years after moving home, I learned how to be patient and kind with myself. I wanted to build a sense of security within myself and, most importantly, focus on healing from my past. I needed to completely and unapologetically focus on myself.

IT WAS ABOUT FINDING THAT HEALTHY BALANCE THAT WORKED FOR US BOTH SO I COULD BE A BETTER PARENT PHYSICALLY AND MENTALLY.

MAM, DAD, CARTER AND ME IN APRIL 2016 WHEN I VERY PROUDLY STOOD BY AOIFE AS HER MAID OF HONOUR DURING HER WEDDING TO RALPH.

Give up giving up

I completed my 12-week food diary and managed to have a loss every single week. Near the end of August, I was down three stone and still in a good headspace. My friends were so supportive of me; any time we planned anything, they made sure that it was somewhere or something that I could enjoy and that worked with my plan. I finally felt like I was in the driver's seat of my own life and heading where I wanted to go. As the weeks went on, losing weight got easier.

I NEEDED TO COMPLETELY AND UNAPOLOGETICALLY FOCUS ON MYSELF.

I got better at saying no. In fact, I felt empowered and in control when I said no to things. I was taking back some of the control over my life. It was a big deal for me, even if it was just my diet. I didn't say no to absolutely everything because I never wanted to feel deprived, so if I really wanted something, I had it, but I tracked it and moved on.

I also became better at recognising and catching old habits creeping in. I used to feel like I messed up my plan by having a treat, so I would have decided to take advantage of the situation and mess up the whole day before starting again. There was a period of time after I first moved home when I was triggered easily: I sometimes had flashbacks when I was on my own, especially at night when I tried to go to sleep. These were times I would have normally relied on food for a distraction and an instant boost of happiness. But I taught myself new habits:

I allowed myself to have those not-so-nice thoughts. I would ground myself and remind myself that that was my past, and I was here today and in control now. If that didn't work, I would go into the kitchen, take out whatever I wanted to binge on, and hold it in my hand to weigh up my options. *Do I want this because I am hungry? Or to cover up the emotions I'm feeling right now?* For the most part, I knew that this piece of food would not fix anything and would satisfy me only momentarily. Still, sometimes I needed the chocolate and would have it – and that worked too!

I was at one of my lowest points when I started, and it wasn't 100 per cent to do with my size. There were many other factors, and I didn't want to feel that way anymore, especially for Carter. So, I focused a lot on my mindset because it's what I struggled with. I stopped thinking about the end goal and started focusing on taking it slow and introducing small changes until they became habits.

Starting is always the hardest because you are already worried about failing. I used to hate telling people when I tried a new diet in case it didn't work out. Constantly thinking of the amount of work I'd have to do is usually what turned me off even starting. So I stopped doing that. I set myself objectives that I knew I was capable of. They didn't have to be drastic. I didn't need to join a gym and train five days a week. I didn't need to cut out certain foods and say no to everything because that's not maintainable or fun for anyone. My objectives were often things like walking to the shops instead of driving, drinking water with every meal, cooking a new recipe from scratch or a new dish once a week. The more consistent I stayed with my objectives, the easier they became, and along the way, I would introduce more and more objectives until they all became habits or part of my daily routine over time. I think the most important thing I did was to give up on giving up. Instead, I took ownership and reminded myself that I was human and that going off-plan never equals failure.

HITTING THE GYM AT THE START OF MY JOURNEY.

Back2Basics

By October 2017, I was down four stone, and Grace convinced me to attend a

personal training session with her in her gym. I had always been so nervous any time I tried to join a gym in the past as it didn't last very long and was never the most positive experience, but Grace reassured me. For some reason, the words 'personal training' intimidated me a little. I had visions of someone standing over me, screaming at me to work harder and faster (it turned out that I couldn't have been more wrong!). She told me it was with a fella named Seán, whom we had briefly hung out with one summer as teenagers. He had a small gym behind his house, and it would only be Grace, him and me. Right after I agreed to go, she decided to tell me that it was at 5.30 a.m.!

So, on the cold morning of 24 October 2017, Grace picked me up and off we went for my first class at Back2Basics Fitness Studio. I hadn't had any gym clothes, so I'd ordered from the men's plus-size range on Asos and was wearing a long-sleeved black top paired with cotton leggings. When we arrived, it was pitch black and freezing cold. We sat in Grace's car and waited for Seán to call us in.

Seán didn't ask me to do anything as outrageous as I had expected. He simply wanted to see my mobility and what I could and couldn't do so that he could create a plan for me. He made me feel completely at ease. He asked me to step forward into a lunge, and, in what felt like slow motion, I dropped to the side and fell on my face. But I was able to laugh at myself. I was a little embarrassed, but not much because I showed up for the next session, and I haven't left Back2Basics alone since.

OF COURSE, IT WOULD BE HARD, BUT THE MORE I DID IT, THE EASIER IT WOULD GET.

I faced my biggest fear by showing up to that gym session. I was so proud of myself for just showing up and trying. And when I would complain about how hard it was for me to do certain movements at home or the fact that I couldn't jog or run because of my weight, Seán would ask me why I was beating myself up about things that I didn't have to do. He always found a way to put a positive spin on everything. He told me to use my extra weight as an advantage: walking and moving with the extra kilos was a workout in itself and was helping me to build muscle. He told me that, instead of worrying about going for a run, I should focus on something as simple as a 15-minute walk in the evening or morning. Of course, it would be hard, but the more I did it, the easier it would get.

For a few months we did personal training together three times a week, and then Seán moved his studio into a huge new warehouse nearby. There were daily classes, but I was terrified to do one. Everyone in the classes looked so fit and fast and knew what they were doing. I still felt like a newbie. But, deep down, a part of me really wanted to do them because I was trying more and more to challenge myself with things outside my comfort zone. Grace and I decided to do one

together. As I was driving to the gym the morning of the class, I felt my phone buzz. As soon as I parked at the gym, I checked my messages, and it was Grace apologising and saying she couldn't make it. My heart sank. I had built myself up so much for this moment, but I couldn't face a class on my own. But Grace was smart and had texted Seán too, and they both knew me well enough to know that I would do a U-turn. Seán walked out of the gym and up to my car.

MY FIRST GYM PARTNER, GRACE, WHO IS HEAVILY PREGNANT HERE WITH HER SON HAYDEN.

'Come on,' he said. 'We will go in together.'

I tried to say no, but he had been so patient with me this entire time, and I had made it this far and knew I would kick myself later. So, I went in. I stood in the first corner I could see and, within minutes, a few girls stood next to me and we started talking. I immediately felt at ease.

Everyone there worked at their own pace and to their own strength. I managed to survive the class; it wasn't half as bad as I'd thought it would be. In fact, after my first class, I was hooked. I started doing them instead of personal training and eventually went to five classes a week. All of the coaches there – Moe, Dean, Shorty and Lewis – couldn't have made me feel more comfortable in my first few weeks of classes. It became one of the most important parts of my day. Every morning, before Carter woke up, I would go there and have my 'me time'. I would get rid of negative energy or thoughts in the classes. Slowly but surely, they were helping to build up my self-esteem.

I gained so much knowledge from each of the trainers about nutrition too – something I didn't really have. In the beginning, my meals were as simple as they could be so that I could stay on track. As I got further into my journey, nutrition became more important to me: I needed to fuel my body with the right foods while training, but it was still important to me that I enjoyed my food and incorporated my favourite meals into my diet to keep me focused and consistent.

My Instagram journey

Around this time, I started my Instagram page, @jens_journey_ie. My friends Grace,

Dominique and Denise had been on social media for years. They were always very confident in front of a camera, but I couldn't have been more different. Anytime we were out somewhere, one of them would whip out their phone and you'd see me dart across the room at ninja speed. I did not like to be on camera. I enjoyed the other side of social media and mainly followed pages that were beneficial to me – lots of foodie ones. I followed many people who would post their meals every day and share different recipe ideas, and I found them so helpful.

CARTER HELPING ME TO WHIP UP SOME RECIPES IN THE KITCHEN. I LOVE INVOLVING HIM IN COOKING AND BAKING WITH MYSELF AND MY MAM.

That January, when I was five stone down, Grace, her sister Mags and I joined a slimming group near us. I finally had the courage to be weighed by someone else. We had the nicest consultant, Miriam, and she allowed me to include the five stone I had already lost. She was always encouraging, and we had a supportive little group. Whenever I shared my meals with them, people often asked for the recipe, so I started taking photographs of my meals one day. When I had my own little collection, I set up a private Instagram page, just for me. It was a great way to keep me accountable, save my recipes and have some fun.

I've always been a visual learner, so it was almost like my food diary but in pictures. It got me excited and encouraged me to think of new recipes. I had the page for weeks before I even told my friends about it, but of course, when I did, they shared it on their own social media pages, and it snowballed from there. I would post my three meals a day and share recipes for meals that were really simple to create and tasty too. I've never been a 'chicken, rice and broccoli every day' kind of girl. I enjoyed thinking up new recipes or whatever I fancied that day; even if that was a takeaway I would recreate it at home in a healthier way – a fakeaway! Many of my meals were convenient, because I didn't have much time to prepare meals or cook overcomplicated dishes in the evenings as a full-time working mammy.

That summer, I was a year into my new lifestyle, and I felt better than ever. My mindset was definitely the slowest part to catch up, especially my inner voice and sense of self-worth. But I allowed myself to be proud of all my progress, especially the non-physical progress that no one could see except me.

My friends didn't realise it then, but their support meant everything to me.

I felt privileged to be surrounded by the most uplifting and inspiring women. They got me through every dark day and let me cry when I needed to (although this was rare because I don't like crying in front of people!). They listened and were always patient with me, even when I'm sure I was hard to be around. My friend Denise and I were both going through difficult times, and we spent close to a year going for a walk together every single night. We made sure we opened up and leaned on each other for support and were lucky that we had each other.

MY FRIENDS DIDN'T REALISE IT THEN, BUT THEIR SUPPORT MEANT EVERYTHING TO ME. I FELT PRIVILEGED TO BE SURROUNDED BY THE MOST UPLIFTING AND INSPIRING WOMEN.

I know that everything happens for a reason but having that support system made me think that if I had gone through what I went through with Eric in Ireland – rather than London – I might not have stayed in that relationship for as long as I did. In London, I grew slowly more isolated from everyone I knew, which made it harder to leave him as I had nowhere to go. I speak to women all the time in similar situations, who have moved away from home or no longer have contact with family and friends and want to leave their abuser but they are isolated and feel very alone, and I know how helpless and scary that can feel. Having a supportive friend is invaluable, and I was so lucky that I had so many.

There will always be people who just don't want to see you happy or see you grow because your happiness reminds them of what they're not doing. That's why the company you keep is so important. Don't ever apologise for being selective about the people you keep around you. Remember, there will always be people who try to hurt you or who are eager to see you fail and that will hurt. It's only human to hurt. But you will grow a thicker skin and learn to not lose sleep over what strangers think.

The simple things

It was a really long time before I could see the weight loss myself. Others saw it before I did. But I would be surprised when my clothes were too big or I needed to drop a size in jeans. The physical change was exciting for me, and not in a vain way. It was exciting to be comfortable enough to walk down the road and not

feel like my size was the first thing people saw. To be in a photograph with friends and not look at it and be the only really big person – I didn't stand out because of my size anymore. That was a big deal for me, because, for about 20 years, I had been afraid of the camera and didn't like anyone taking a picture of me, ever. Suddenly, I was happy to smile for a picture. I was able to go shopping with my friends and look at clothes I liked in regular clothes shops rather than the clothes that fit me in only a handful of shops. There were so many things I was enjoying about life that I hadn't before. I went on my first girls' holiday in a long time. My friends from home – Aoife, Emer, Niamh – and I went to Bucharest for a few days, and it was one of my favourite trips ever. I fully immersed myself in every part of it and felt completely content. We laughed from start to finish, and I had only just started to gain confidence and be more present in the moment rather than in my head worrying.

People always ask me what the biggest or best change I've noticed since losing weight is. My life then and now are incomparable, and I have always been grateful to my body throughout my entire journey – but now I was able to do so many things that I'd wanted to do. I had a new energy inside and a whole new attitude.

I found an interest in hobbies that I had never imagined myself doing because of fear and social insecurities. But the biggest changes for me were the smallest things, simple things that I never even

ON HOLIDAY IN FUERTEVENTURA IN 2018. THIS WAS THE FIRST HOLIDAY I WENT ON WHERE I FELT COMFORTABLE IN MY CLOTHES AND IN MYSELF.

realised I had been missing out on: walking down the field with Carter and a football, running around and not wasting a minute worrying about how I looked or people seeing me, being able to go for a bike ride with him without worrying about breaking the bike or having zero energy to keep up. Of course, anybody can do most, if not all, of these things, regardless of their size – but I never did them when I was bigger. I know it's sad, unhealthy and wrong to think that way, but I did. I held myself back from everything because of my size. I try not to dwell on it because I've grown from it, but I do regret how much time I wasted worrying about my size and what other people might be thinking. For 20-plus years, that's how my mind worked. I think of all of that time wasted and what I could have been spending it on. You need to live your life for yourself and for no one else. Your life won't be your own if you're constantly worrying or caring about what other people are thinking.

I TRY NOT TO DWELL ON IT BECAUSE I'VE GROWN FROM IT, BUT I DO REGRET HOW MUCH TIME I WASTED WORRYING ABOUT MY SIZE AND WHAT OTHER PEOPLE MIGHT BE THINKING.

My inspiration

Having Carter gave me a new purpose: a new reason to want to live life to the fullest. He inspired me every day just by being his little self. He was my ray of sunshine on my darkest days, and I owe him so much of my strength because he helped me find it. It's hard to talk about him without sounding like a cheesy Hallmark card, but I don't know where I would be if it wasn't for him.

CARTER AND ME CELEBRATING HIS THIRD BIRTHDAY IN MAY 2018. HE HELPED ME BAKE A HUGE CAKE, AND WE HAD A GARDEN PARTY WITH FRIENDS AND FAMILY.

I remember my friend Niamh telling me, 'Against all odds, he was supposed to come into your life exactly when he did and teach you all that he has.' And she was right; I wouldn't be here today if it wasn't for him. I wish I could say that I

CARTER AND ME AT THE CLIFFS OF MOHER IN AUGUST 2021. WE WENT ON A TWO-WEEK HOLIDAY AROUND THE WEST OF IRELAND, JUST THE TWO OF US.

loved myself enough or that I was worth making the positive changes for. But I never respected myself or loved myself enough to want to change my life for me. I didn't feel deserving. When Carter came along, I finally discovered something inside me that I had never had before: a determination to do anything that would better his life and mine. I hate even hearing myself say that because I still feel riddled with guilt. But the first year or two of Carter's life was the hardest time on my own. What should have been the happiest, most loving years hold so much pain for me. He is the best thing that ever happened to me, and he has made my life a million times more fulfilling, but I hate that I have so many sad and painful memories attached to that time too. I feel robbed of what should have been a special time with only wonderful, happy memories. But I remind myself daily that we get to make each year together better and better. I wouldn't be the parent or the person I am today if I didn't take the path that I did, and I might not have the same relationship that I have with Carter today. I am always grateful for our strong bond.

Sometimes the unimaginably hard things that we go through in life put us on a path to the most wonderful things that will ever happen. The painful things we experience are not always burdens; they are gifts that give us the ability to discover what we are capable of. And that's exactly what Carter was: a wonderful gift and the beginning of the rest of my life.

My motivation

A year on, I hit my 10-stone goal. I couldn't believe it. This was the day I didn't even like to think about a year before, because I wasn't sure I would ever get there. It was a huge achievement to me because I proved to myself that I was not a failure and that when I believed in myself and encouraged myself, I got to see a little of what I was made of. In the past, I had never made it this far into a new lifestyle. There was always something that would drag me back, and I would give up on myself, blaming my lack of motivation.

You don't learn how to be motivated one day, and that's it. It requires persistent digging and pushing. And it will go. There will always be times when you lose it, and perhaps your priorities change, but what's important is that when you want it again, you set your intentions and get to work. I remained consistent in the gym and aimed for five days a week. I loved it more than ever. It was my daily therapy.

Around this time, I moved away from slimming clubs. I had done a year with them, and they had helped me lose most of my weight by breaking food down into a handful of simplified categories. It made for a straightforward, easy plan for me to follow. I spoke to my coaches about it, and at the time, Seán was keen for me to do whatever worked for me and made me happy. But I knew that he wasn't a fan of these slimming groups as there was not much nutritional information being shared, and that's such a big part of a lifestyle change. The more weight I lost and the more I trained, the more interested I became in eating a leaner, higher-protein diet. I was conscious of what I was putting into my body – not to an extreme, but I wanted to make better choices day to day. My coaches gave me a better understanding of the importance of food when training.

YOU DON'T LEARN HOW TO BE MOTIVATED ONE DAY, AND THAT'S IT. IT REQUIRES PERSISTENT DIGGING AND PUSHING.

So, I decided to leave my slimming club on a high after my 10-stone award, and to trust myself to carry on with the support of my coaches when I needed them. Investing in a professional when it comes to nutrition and training is the best way to educate yourself. I was excited about the change and felt very lucky to have five of the best mentors around. Changing over to calorie-counting was a bit of a learning curve, but I enjoyed the challenge. I just didn't enjoy how much longer it took to work out the calories when cooking from scratch! But after a few weeks, armed with a calorie calculator

on my phone, I could do it with my eyes closed. Since it became second nature to me and the recipes were helping me so much, I thought they could be helpful to others, too. I was still very much focused on tasty, achievable and family-friendly meals, but I also wanted to incorporate more nutritional, high-protein and simple meals.

HEADING OUT FOR ST PATRICK'S DAY, ALMOST A FULL YEAR INTO MY JOURNEY. I WAS BEGINNING TO SEE A CHANGE IN MYSELF, MENTALLY, PHYSICALLY AND EMOTIONALLY.

I started to share my meals' calories on my social media as well. I had become much more active on my social media, speaking to the camera and showing my face. For the first few months, I hadn't shown myself, so a lot of people following me had no idea what I looked or sounded like. It's hard to keep a genuine rapport with people following you when they have no idea who you are, so, one day, I decided to say hello, and since then, I haven't shut up. I'm so glad I did because my social media platform has opened many doors and brought me many amazing opportunities. It has also helped me push the boundaries on things that I never thought I would do. I had been so self-conscious about my size, so openly discussing my weight with thousands of people online was very liberating.

I decided to open up about my past too. I was always asked about my weight loss journey and what triggered me to start when I did. I felt like I couldn't give a true answer without talking about why we moved home and the abuse I had faced because it all led me to where I was. When I opened up about it, a lot of family and friends had had no idea what had gone on, so it was a shock for them.

I HAD BEEN SO SELF-CONSCIOUS ABOUT MY SIZE, SO OPENLY DISCUSSING MY WEIGHT WITH THOUSANDS OF PEOPLE ONLINE WAS VERY LIBERATING.

There has always been a stigma attached to domestic violence. Often, victims can feel ashamed or be conditioned to believe that they have brought their abuse upon themselves and so it's not often something we hear being spoken about openly. I wanted to share what had happened to me so that it might help others who have been there – or are there – to feel less alone and to show people that this can happen to anyone. I remember, when I was in my situation, it was the loneliest I've ever been. Even though domestic abuse stats are dangerously high, you feel as though you're the only person in the world going through it at that moment and that nobody else has any idea what you are living with. Being able to use my platform to raise awareness for victims of domestic abuse is the thing I am most proud of. I put myself at my most vulnerable and opened up in the hope of encouraging others to do the same and to know that there is always help available. It doesn't 'get better' on its own, and you can always reach out to professional people and ask for help no matter what. There is life after abuse; you will never need to live in shame.

EVEN THOUGH DOMESTIC ABUSE STATS ARE DANGEROUSLY HIGH, YOU FEEL AS THOUGH YOU'RE THE ONLY PERSON IN THE WORLD GOING THROUGH IT AT THAT MOMENT AND THAT NOBODY ELSE HAS ANY IDEA WHAT YOU ARE LIVING WITH.

I was so overwhelmed by the response I got. So many people, mostly strangers, reached out to me and shared their stories. I got a lot of opportunities to speak publicly around Ireland about my experience. At first, I said no, because public speaking is very different from sitting in your bedroom talking to your phone. But the more I thought about it, the more I realised that it was bigger than me and my little fear. I imagined the one person who might be unsure about their own situation in a room full of women. I am not saying that I thought I was going to inspire people to make changes. But the idea that maybe someone needed to just hear another person talk about something they were currently experiencing, and that that might make them feel a little more hopeful, was enough to push me to do it. I kept thinking of myself attending a similar talk when I was in my relationship and how it would have been nice just to feel a little less alone. For the first time ever, I was having real-time conversations with real people who had been through the same thing I had. I had never had that before, and opening up to these women was a big part of my healing process. Naturally, Carter was always at the forefront of my mind. I second-guessed myself a lot when I decided to come out about the abuse. Even as I write this book, I worry about how permanent it is and how it's both of our lives that I am sharing. I could go back and forth all day wondering if it's the right choice, but I always circle back to the same thought: raising awareness, helping others and trying to work together to lift the stigma on domestic abuse is bigger

than our story. We have no shame, and in putting it out there I can only hope that when Carter is older he understands why I spoke up about my abuse and that he will be proud.

Trust the process

〃

WHEN YOU GIVE YOURSELF A SPECIFIC NUMBER, YOU PUT SO MUCH PRESSURE ON YOURSELF TO REACH AND MAINTAIN THAT NUMBER.

〃

Two years into my journey, I had managed to lose 12 stone and keep it off. I fluctuated maybe 7 lbs on each side, depending on what was going on in my life. Getting comfortable with fluctuation, especially as a woman, is so important. It is very easy to get obsessed with the scales and allow them to control your happiness. On a weight-loss journey, especially at the beginning, we often see significant losses and celebrate them and our hard work. But when the losses become less frequent, and we begin to maintain or gain, we can feel disappointed in ourselves. We can feel that we didn't work hard enough and must work even harder the following week for a loss. Sometimes, the more weight you lose, the scales stop moving or start to move at an incredibly slow rate. Usually, that means that your body has adapted to your calories and you're now in maintenance and, for me, this is when my coaches come in and adjust my calories.

But it's important to recognise that every day you do your best, your best will look different. Doing your best won't always feel the same and you won't always achieve the same outcome. You can't allow the scales to define your happiness or hard work. Our bodies fluctuate for a hundred different reasons – that's just science! If you're eating well and actively moving your body, you need to trust the process; the scales will always catch up.

From the start, one thing I never did was give myself a target weight. I think target weights are unrealistic for most people and can do more damage. Yes, I may have a rough figure where I feel most comfortable on the scales, but I always give 5 to 7 lbs on each side, because that is how I fluctuate. When you give yourself a specific number, you put so much pressure on yourself to reach and maintain that number. The scale is a great tool if you need it or want it to track, but that is all it is: a tool. If you connect too much emotion to it, or it triggers you or causes an eating disorder, you should ditch the scales. You want to be eating right and exercising to feel like the best version of you: full of energy and happy

endorphins. Not just so you can see the same number on the scales every morning. I still have moments when I get frustrated with the scales, but once I recognise this in myself, I take a step back and remind myself of the above. If I feel frustrated, I ask myself, *Did I have a good week? Before weighing myself, did I feel good?* And if the answer is yes, then I move on unbothered; if the answer is no, then it is most likely to do with my cycle!

I AM WAITING TO HAVE THE EXCESS SKIN REMOVED FROM MY LEGS. I AM EXCITED FOR THAT PART OF MY JOURNEY TO BE OVER, BUT I ALSO APPRECIATE HOW FAR I HAVE COME AND THE HARD WORK I HAVE PUT IN.

Letting go

YOU HAVE THE ENTIRE YEAR TO FUEL YOUR BODY WITH NUTRITIOUS FOODS AND EXERCISE REGULARLY; A WEEK OR A COUPLE WEEKS HERE AND THERE WILL NOT UNDO THE WORK YOU'VE ALREADY DONE.

I get so many messages around Christmas and summertime from people who are genuinely upset because they have 'let themselves go' and gained weight. I hate that term 'let yourself go'. Where do you go? You were celebrating with friends and family and enjoying life, good food and perhaps alcohol. Isn't that what life's all about? Celebrating and being merry together when we can, living in the moment and making memories. How boring would life be if we took all of that away? In the last few years, I've always made sure that I enjoy special occasions like holidays. I remember Carter and my first holiday together on our own in 2018. We went to San Juan in Spain for seven

days and I came home 18 lbs heavier! But I got myself back into my normal routine, and two or three weeks later, it was gone. As I mentioned, I fluctuate a lot; I can go to bed and wake up 4 lbs heavier. That's just my body, and I have learned how it works. I knew I didn't gain 18 lbs of fat in seven days. There were loads of other things to consider there, so I didn't panic when I saw the number on the scales. I also didn't continue eating what I wanted all day. I returned to my usual routine of planning meals and sticking to my calories.

CARTER AND I WENT ON HOLIDAY TO SAN JUAN, SPAIN, AND HAD THE BEST TIME TOGETHER, JUST THE TWO OF US.

It's the same at Christmas: I don't think about calories or better choices for a good chunk of December. It doesn't mean that every single day for the month of December I'll eat chocolate for breakfast. But on days when I want to go for dinner and drinks or sit on the couch and eat turkey sandwiches and graze the tin of Roses, I do it. Because on the other

AOIFE, ME, NIAMH AND EMER IN 2019.

days of the month, I make healthier choices. It doesn't have to be all or nothing. There are 31 days in December, which gives us 93 meals (breakfast, lunch and dinner), so even if we had 33 of those meals out with friends or at home and off-plan, we still have 60 of them for which we can make more conscious choices. Remind yourself that you can always start tomorrow, that life is never consistent, and neither will your diet be. So, if you decide to take the month of December off because that works for you, then you know best. You have the entire year to fuel your body with nutritious foods and exercise regularly; a week or a couple weeks here and there will not undo the work you've already done. Years down the line, what do you think you will remember more – the memories you made during Christmas or the last week of November when you were a few pounds lighter on the scales? We all need to find our healthy balance, and once you have that, you lose a lot of the guilt and worry associated with weight fluctuation.

The Moe mindset

WORKING OUT IN THE BACK2BASICS GYM.

From the beginning of my journey, I knew that excess skin was something I was going to be left with. It's impossible to know how much or how little you will have, but usually, the more weight you lose, the more skin you'll be left with. I also knew that no amount of exercise would prevent it because of how much excess skin I would have. Before I began my surgery journey, it was important to me that I was in the best shape possible – and so along came Moe to be my personal trainer. I thought it would be a good idea to have personal training in the run-up to my surgeries and afterwards, while I was recovering, to ensure that I was doing everything as I should. I knew that I was in great hands with Moe because I had been training with him for two years in the group classes, and he was a fantastic coach. What I didn't know was how much I would learn from Moe and about myself through working with him one-on-one. I knew that I struggled with confidence and body positivity, but I didn't realise how bad I was. I have always said that losing weight was the easy part for me; changing my mindset and how I speak to myself has been the hardest. I thought that I had got so much better at it over the years, and I would tell people that I had – but I hadn't. Sometimes I said something without even realising that I was putting myself down. Moe would pull me up on it every single time. As a coach, he's very much about attitude and mental wellbeing. I check in with him weekly and will track everything from calories and protein to sleep and steps. But the most important part of our check-ins are the voice notes when I tell him about my week: what I got up to, how I was feeling, my energy, if anything not-so-good happened – basically as much or as little detail as I want. (Obviously, with me he gets an hour-by-hour recap of my week!)

When we first started working together, my goal was to drop fat and gain muscle before surgery, and instead of making me focus solely on calories and protein, Moe made me look at other areas: small goals or things that I could do to improve my confidence. Other times, he might set me challenges – like whenever I said something negative about myself, for example, I had to do five burpees. I think I did about 50 in one session. It really opened my eyes to how often I criticised myself and how rarely, if ever, I complimented myself. Together we've worked a lot on my way of thinking, and while I am nowhere near where I want to be, I am okay knowing that I am a work in progress. It's important to Moe that his clients look at the bigger picture, not just the physical change. He tells me all the time how proud I should be when I look at how far I have come – not just the weight loss, but all the knowledge I have gained in the last few years from my experiences. Moe reminds me all the time that it really isn't all about the outcome and final results, it's much more to do with the journey and the process: what we learn about ourselves along the way, the little changes and rituals we put in place for ourselves and how we adapt our lifestyles to make them work. He has given me the five pillars of positivity that I always go back to. They are things that I want to be focusing on in my life. They change from time to time, but whenever I am having a tough day or week, he tells me to read

over them to remind myself of why I am doing what I am doing.

Sometimes I don't think I have changed that much. I still doubt my ability and keep my guard up to protect myself. I still forget that my strength and resilience are two of my strongest characteristics. I often don't allow myself to go for things because I am afraid it will jeopardise how far I have come and that I'll go back to a time when I felt helpless and unable. But then I remember that I am more than my past and that I have grown through these experiences and gained the knowledge and tools that help me recognise these emotions. So, I allow myself to feel them and then learn and grow more from them. I know that if myself from 10 years ago met the version I am today, she would not recognise me. Of course, I'm still the same Jen, but I have changed drastically: not just in terms of the weight I carried, but my ways of thinking, my ability to listen, my empathy, my patience, my strength, my boundaries, my compassion, my honesty, my integrity and my core values have all been strengthened. I have grown so much that some days I have to remind myself of that and that it's good to be proud of myself.

My point is that – even when we don't realise it, or when it doesn't feel like it – every hard challenge we face, every regret we have, every difficult decision and every heartbreak gets us to where we are. We heal, we learn and we grow. So even when you feel as though not much is changing, just know that you need to trust the process. Everything is unfolding for you just as it should.

Moe helped me develop a new way of thinking regarding my progress, because so much of it is linked to all the factors in my life. It's not black and white, and there's never a reason to rush it. Although I still have a long way to go, I have grown so much already in my self-esteem and confidence. As a result of working with Moe before the surgery, not only did I feel physically ready, I felt mentally ready.

Making a decision

Surgery had always been something I saw happening for myself when I was ready. Surgery is a massive and very personal decision, and when I opened up about it online, a few people messaged me to say that I should spend the money on therapy and learn about self-love. I didn't really agree with that one. I don't think cosmetic surgery and self-love are mutually exclusive, the same way that loving your body and still wanting to lose weight aren't. I think it's easy to have an opinion on something you don't understand. After losing 12 stone and carrying that excess skin around for a long time, I knew it was the right thing for me. Not only is the skin incredibly uncomfortable, but I also hated looking at it. Some people love and embrace their excess skin, and that's beautiful. But I didn't, and I knew I never would. Simple as. I did have a lot of it, and I always will

have excess skin because I'm not having surgery on every inch of my body, and there's only so much that can be done in the areas where I did have surgery.

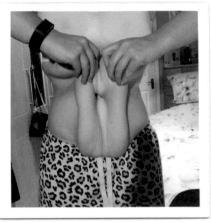

THE NIGHT BEFORE MY FLEUR-DE-LIS SURGERY. I WAS A BAG OF EMOTIONS WHEN LEAVING CARTER BEFORE THE SURGERY, BUT I WAS REALLY EXCITED TO FINALLY BE RID OF THAT EXCESS SKIN.

Carrying around the excess weight is uncomfortable, especially with the kind of training I do. I found many exercises painful or embarrassing due to my excess skin. I would never say it in class at the time and would always try my best. For four years, I worked consistently at Back2Basics. I never dipped in and out. I made it a part of my day-to-day routine and will continue to do so. It was tough training five days a week for years, and even though I felt a hundred times better, it was disheartening that I was left with a massive amount of excess skin. I knew, and my trainers knew, that no matter how much training I did, the only way I could get rid of my skin would be to have it surgically removed.

A PICTURE I NEVER THOUGHT I WOULD SHARE. THIS WAS RIGHT BEFORE MY SURGERIES, AND IT WAS SO HARD FOR ME TO LOOK AT MYSELF EVERY DAY LIKE THIS WITH ALL OF THE WORK I HAD PUT IN.

MY WEIGHT-LOSS JOURNEY HAS BEEN MUCH QUICKER THAN MY CONFIDENCE AND SELF-ESTEEM JOURNEY, AND AT THIS POINT, THOSE FEELINGS HAD ONLY JUST BEEN LIFTED OFF THE FLOOR.

I felt like I deserved it. I had worked hard and wanted to be able to see some of my results. The parts that caused the most pain were my legs, tummy and back. They moved a lot when I did, and

especially when I exercised. In hot weather, all that excess skin was uncomfortable. I could hide it well under clothes, and people would always say, 'You look great. You don't look like you need surgery!' But it was all there, and I had to look at it every day. It was harder to cover up in hotter weather, especially on holidays. Now that I had lost weight, I could fit into lots of clothes I liked, but I still opted for the ones that covered my skin. The excess skin on my arms was probably the least painful, but I was very self-conscious about it. I have quite big arms naturally, and after the weight loss, the skin on them was very obvious. Before my weight loss, I always feared shopping for clothes, and this didn't go away entirely after I lost the weight. Shopping to hide my excess skin was just as frustrating for me. And I know I didn't have to hide it, but that was how I felt.

My weight-loss journey has been much quicker than my confidence and self-esteem journey, and at this point, those feelings had only just been lifted off the floor. Even wearing a T-shirt, the skin would hang down past my elbows, and it looked strange. It's hard to explain, but my whole life, I had looked in the mirror and hated what I saw looking back at me. After losing all the weight, I expected to look in the mirror every day and love what I saw – but I didn't, and that was almost harder. When I looked at myself before the weight loss, I saw someone who was big, but now the skin I was left with on every part of my body looked abnormal to me. I don't want to offend anyone, but that was just honestly how I felt. I had never seen a body like that before, and I worked so hard that it was tough to still have such negative feelings about my body. Yes, I was so grateful and proud, but I didn't love what I saw and knew that I probably never would. That's okay; I wasn't going to beat myself up for not loving what I saw. But I had the opportunity to change it through surgery and was more than happy to do so.

The only issue was that, when I tried to do my research on it, I couldn't find very much. The clinics were always based in the UK, the USA or Australia. I followed many people on social media who had had the surgeries done that I wanted, but they were all abroad.

After many hours of research, I finally decided that I would have my surgery done at the Avoca Clinic in Wicklow. The first surgery would be on my stomach. It was called a fleur-de-lis, designed to remove a significant amount of skin from the midsection. It would leave two scars: one would be horizontal, similar to a standard tummy tuck scar, and the other would run vertically up the stomach, creating an upside-down uppercase T, or a fleur-de-lis symbol. I found a surgeon at the Avoca Clinic who had performed this particular surgery and had a good reputation. The surgery was expensive, but having it in Ireland was one of my top priorities. I had savings and it was going to be worth every penny.

However, even after booking my surgery, I would have moments of doubt where I would think, *What if my real issue is with self-love?* But I reminded myself that as long as I was doing it completely for me and for my own needs and happiness, I had not rushed into an idea.

I booked my consultation at the Avoca in the spring of 2019. As soon as I arrived, I felt very comfortable and excited. My mam came with me so that I felt more at ease. I had a notepad and a list of questions for my surgeon. I had never been to this clinic before, so I had assumed that it was like a mini hospital, but the reception and waiting area were very fancy. There were fresh flowers everywhere and pretty-smelling candles that helped me to relax. My surgeon reviewed my skin and was very honest with me, which I appreciated. He explained that I had been left with an awful lot of excess skin, and that even with a fleur-de-lis surgery I would still have some excess left at my upper tummy and a lot on my back. We both agreed that a '360 degree' surgery, where you are turned over mid-surgery, was riskier. I knew there would be a time when the fleur-de-lis would need revision.

He also agreed that my legs were left with a tremendous amount of skin and that this was a surgery we would need to discuss down the line, after the fleur-de-lis, as it would be a big surgery. After my consultation, I felt comfortable and confident and excited that it felt like it was finally happening for me. I didn't leave Avoca Clinic that day without booking my surgery date and paying my deposit!

The big day

u

I COULDN'T GET OVER THE FEELING OF STANDING STRAIGHT AND NOT HAVING ANY BELLY, SKIN OR FAT HANGING DOWN.

u

On 16 July 2019, I had my surgery and spent one night in hospital. When I woke up from the surgery, I couldn't believe how small my waist looked. It was bandaged up, but I could still see how different it looked. I started to cry happy tears. I just remember feeling incredibly proud; it was a moment I had never even imagined for myself. I was pretty high on medication too! I called the nurse to help me go to the bathroom. She waited outside the door, and I remember I just couldn't help myself when I was looking in the mirror. I opened the Velcro on my waist compression garment and looked in the mirror. I couldn't get over the feeling of standing straight and not having any belly, skin or fat hanging down. That was all I had seen in the mirror for as long as I could remember – so this was surreal. I remember putting my hand on my stomach and it feeling so alien. Where I was touching my tummy and waist was a part of me that I hadn't felt before. The only way I can describe it was almost like my head hadn't caught up with my body, and feeling like it wasn't my body – and all of a sudden, I felt so sick and dizzy and collapsed in the toilet. Luckily, the nurse caught me just as I went down and she managed to get me back into the bed. I was grand with a few glasses of water, but it was a strange sensation that I'll never forget.

u

AGAIN, I FELT VULNERABLE SHARING SUCH INTIMATE IMAGES AND DETAILS, BUT I REMEMBERED HOW HARD I HAD FOUND IT TO FIND INFORMATION ON THESE KINDS OF SURGERIES IN IRELAND.

u

The pain for everyone varies so much on these surgeries. I was lucky enough to find mine quite manageable and, of course, stayed on top of my pain medication. I felt more uncomfortable than sore, with a tightness that made me hunch over. I decided to document my entire surgery journey on my social media platforms, an idea I had toyed with for a little while. Again, I felt vulnerable sharing such intimate images and details, but I remembered how hard I had found it to find information on these kinds of surgeries in Ireland. I knew there must be other people in the same situation as me who would also like to know more or possibly have the same surgeries. So, I shared it all. And I'm so glad I did because the response I got from the public was so positive. So many people reached out – men and women of all ages who had struggled to hide excess skin for years and never knew what kind of options were available.

During my recovery, I had some time off to rest and I connected with lots of people online and had lots of conversations with people who had the same questions and worries I had. I tried my best to rest as much as I could and, luckily, I had my parents there to help me. I had also meal-prepped a lot the week before my surgery and had meals to hand when I was unable to move around and cook. When I was preparing them, I knew I would thank myself later – and I did! I cooked a lot of high-protein meals packed with vegetables, with good fats and rich in iron. Batch-cooking meals such as curries, chilli con carne and pasta dishes were all very handy as they were easy to reheat and so filling. I think fuelling myself well after the surgery helped a lot with my healing.

A couple of weeks later, I got invited to a morning breakfast show on live television to share my story. I was so nervous. I was still very swollen and had quite a bit of pain with two huge drains hanging out of me, with litre bottles on the end of each one, which were full of ... gross fluids! I wore a long dress and tucked the bottles under the sofa during the interview. I was so proud of myself for doing that too. I felt like I was facing so many fears and saying yes to everything I would normally say no to. Someone who is trained in acting being apprehensive about going on TV might sound bizarre, but it's completely different when you are going on as yourself and talking about your real life. I remember my surgeon at that time said he had never had so many inquiries about a fleur-de-lis as he did in the few weeks after I shared my story.

ON HOLIDAY IN LANZAROTE IN AUGUST 2022. IT WAS THE FIRST TIME I WORE A BIKINI – AGED 33. IT WAS A REALLY BIG DEAL FOR ME.

My six weeks of recovery went smoothly, and when they were up, I went straight back to the gym, according to the plan Moe and I had developed. I already couldn't wait for my next surgery.

As time went on, the results got better and better. After about a year,

I could feel and see the excess skin at the top of my stomach and back, as the surgeon at the Avoca Clinic had said there would be. I wanted to give myself and that area at least a full year to heal before revisiting. I decided that I would have the surgery on my arms done next and would have a breast lift at the same time. My surgeon at the clinic was happy to do both of the surgeries in one. I opted against a breast implant, even though most advised it would give a better result because I didn't have much fat left to work with. I was happy to go ahead and have smaller breasts. At one point, I had been a G-cup, so I really didn't mind being smaller going into my thirties.

This surgery took place the following September, in 2020 – a little later than expected, as the Covid-19 pandemic hit the world that year and we needed to be careful and follow guidelines. I was glad to be having both my arms and breasts done at the same time. When I woke up following the surgery, I remember thinking that my boobs still looked really big. I was confused and wondered if they had mistakenly put an implant in! But it was just the swelling, and they settled down over time.

My breasts were the easiest and least painful surgery, recovery-wise. My arms, however, were extremely sore after surgery as they were so tight, and you need to constantly move your arms. The surgeon explained that my arms would need a little revision as they hadn't been able to remove all of the skin in that one surgery. Again, my recovery went smoothly, and it was so nice to have an

arm I could wave without feeling so much heavy skin flopping around!

I went back to have my revision done and to discuss my final surgeries: my legs and back. There was a new surgeon at the Avoca, who had been there for a little while. I had been following his work and just knew that he was the surgeon I wanted to do my final two surgeries. I met with Dr Cormac Joyce and was so excited by how enthusiastic he was about my surgeries. He talked to me about the places he had trained around the world and who he had studied with. He had a real passion for his work and seemed to specialise in the kind of surgeries I was after. Excess skin extended leg surgery is not commonly done in Ireland. Again, it's really hard to research because not many people have had it. But Dr Joyce reassured me and was open to trying different things I had asked.

Scars don't bother me a lot, but I know many people are conscious of them and surgeons will keep this in mind. I had a lot of skin around my knees, making the surgery more complex. Dr Joyce explained to me how he could remove a large amount of it but that I would be left with visible scars. I would rather have scars than the skin. I was so eager to have Dr Joyce do the surgeries that I asked him to do my revision on both my arms and stomach, and he agreed. This time, when he did my fleur-de-lis, he did the muscle repair for my stomach. He explained that with dissolvable stitches there would be absolutely no issue if I became pregnant in the future. I had no liposuction or 4D (which involves using liposuction along muscular lines to create the appearance of more defined abs) work on my tummy, which Dr Joyce specialises in, but the results were incredible.

"

IN THE SIX WEEKS BEFORE MY SURGERIES, I MAKE SURE MY DIET IS AS GOOD AS IT CAN BE.

"

The muscle repair made this recovery the hardest I had ever had. I think I had 8cm of muscle that had been stretched over the years through weight gain and then split through pregnancy. For the first two weeks, I could not stand up straight, laugh, cough or sneeze because the pain was so bad. When I did need to cough, the fear that came over me was so intense that all I could do was laugh! That became a daily occurrence that was fun for my mam to watch but less so for me to endure.

I think a huge part of why my recoveries seem to go well is how much I train and how active I am. In the six weeks before my surgeries, I make sure my diet is as good as it can be. I try to fuel my body with as many nutrients and as much protein as possible. In the week leading up to surgery, I'll usually up my training a little more where I have time and focus on more nutritious meals. I have a good balance of lean proteins, carbohydrates,

good fats and plenty of vegetables (especially the greens!). I usually avoid alcohol as far as possible – not completely, but I wouldn't have lots of big nights out where drinking is involved. I prepare a lot of my meals and freeze some so that I have them to hand during recovery too. When my body is healing for the first few days, I usually stick to tea and toast, but as soon as I come round and start feeling less groggy, I make sure that I'm eating good meals; this always helps my energy levels and makes me feel a little more like myself.

After the operation, I listen to my body and, of course, my surgeon's advice. As soon as I feel able and have been given the clear, I head straight to my PT for a week or so before going back to my classes. Moe will always start with very basic, minimal movements, just to see what I'm capable of, and when I go back to classes, I always go at my own pace. But every time, I surprise myself with how quickly I fall back into it and just how amazing our bodies can be at bouncing back. Immediately after surgery, I feel like I'll never be able to step foot in the gym again, but you surprise yourself with how quickly that feeling goes. After each of my surgeries, I've been back to my regular class and routine within two months.

The best advice I can give someone is to listen to your body and rest as much as you can in the first couple of weeks after surgery. When people offer to help or cook, don't be a typical Irish person and decline the help! I was lucky enough that I had my parents to help with Carter for the first week or two post-op. You definitely need extra support, especially if you have little ones. I also found it easy to fall into a habit of eating convenient comfort food. The first few days are fine as your appetite is usually smaller than normal, but it's handy to prepare meals for yourself pre-surgery so that you can then grab them from the freezer every day and have a tasty, healthy meal ready. I found that, because I wasn't walking or moving at all for a couple of weeks, I needed the nutrients to keep my energy and my mood up and to aid my recovery.

After my second surgery, I discovered lymphatic drainage massage, which helped massively with my recovery. Most patients are aware that swelling is going to be a huge part of their recovery for a long time; some people even find it lasts three to six months after surgery. I normally wait about five days and then have two lymphatic drainage massages a week for three or four weeks, depending on whether I need them or not. This technique is a very soft, stroking-like massage that relieves painful swelling. I feel instantly better after it, as the swelling can be incredibly uncomfortable. After the first few weeks, the swelling is still there for me, but it's not as painful. I always find that I don't see the true results of surgery until about 6 to 12 months later.

I began my surgery journey in 2019 and had hoped to be finished with it in 2021, but due to Covid-19, my remaining surgeries were pushed back. As I write this book, I am preparing for my final surgeries in the spring of 2023: to my legs and my back and underarm area. I am so excited to finally be nearing the end of my surgery journey. It's been a long few years, but it was the best thing I ever did for my self-esteem. I enjoy training so much more now, as a lot of the discomfort is gone, and I know that after my legs, I won't know myself.

What's next?

I always get asked what's next once my surgeries are done – and honestly, I have no idea! I am just really looking forward to having the bulk of my excess skin gone and focusing on maintaining the lifestyle I have created for myself. I enjoy sharing things I find helpful online, and I'm sure I'll still be on Instagram telling you about the calories in a healthy, yummy spice bag or sharing videos of me throwing myself around the gym. Like life, my goals change all the time. I am sure there will be times when I want to get a little leaner or drop some extra weight. There will also be times when I'm just happy maintaining the weight I am at and enjoying the lifestyle I have. One thing I know is that I won't ever lose my passion for training and the happy balance I have found in my diet.

I am still – and will consistently be – on a journey to self-love and confidence. I want the kind of confidence where I don't feel the need to compare myself to anyone. Whenever I feel like I haven't learned a thing, I look back on each year over the last four years and almost can't recognise the woman I was when I began. So even though this journey of self-love is taking a lot longer than I might have imagined, I don't mind because I have learned to trust both the process and myself. I know how much I want to get better at it, and I believe that I will get there. I began to believe in myself when I was at my lowest, which got me to where I am today. I didn't want to make these changes to be as good as or better than anyone else; I wanted to be the best for Carter and for me. I wanted to be proud of myself and prove to myself that I did have the strength inside me to make the changes I wanted. I had been through so much trauma in a short space of time, and I was still here. I faced all that alone and walked away with my head held high. So, deep down, I knew I had it in me. I just needed to be my own biggest cheerleader and remind myself that I was capable when I doubted myself.

I AM STILL – AND WILL CONSISTENTLY BE – ON A JOURNEY TO SELF-LOVE AND CONFIDENCE.

I changed a lot about my life in a short space of time and I can't wait to see what the next four years have in store for me. I get asked a lot about trust and moving on into a new serious relationship. I do hope that that is a part of our future,

and I know that if it happens, I will take my time. I worry that no one will ever love me because of my past. I don't know why I think this way, because I would never feel that way about someone else's past, but the fear of meeting a new person plays on my mind a lot. I lost the little confidence I had in myself at the hands of someone else, and I sometimes find it difficult to see myself ever being able to trust completely again. I have a guard up, and I've tried to let it down and let people in, but as soon as I feel like they're gonna hurt me, I back down completely. I think that I naturally assume that the worst is going to happen, so I prepare myself for it to happen. Even when there are no red flags, I constantly expect one to appear. I have a guard up to protect myself from getting hurt. But this applies to all the relationships I have in my life. I often see small traits that I have worked hard on losing creeping back in. Especially pleasing people. But at least I now recognise when I do this. I have so much more self-worth than I did before, making it a lot easier to see when I am putting myself in a situation that I don't need or want to be in. It is one of the traits that I have found hardest to stop completely.

One thing that helps me with people-pleasing tendencies are healthy boundaries. Creating boundaries is the easy part; staying consistent with them is usually where most people struggle. If I don't have these boundaries in place, I can very easily begin to feel resentment towards people. Holding on to that resentment over time only builds up and up, making a situation much worse than it needs to be. The more I practise establishing boundaries, the easier it becomes and the stronger I feel. It gives me more control in situations where I otherwise might feel pressured to give in to something I don't want to. When I am doing something for someone else that I don't particularly want to do, I listen to my inner voice, and I ask myself if I'm doing it because I want to or because I don't want to upset the other person or hurt their feelings by saying no, and I remind myself that my needs are important too. They need to be put first more often than not, and this allows me to say yes to myself a lot more, which has a big positive effect on my emotional well-being. Learning to say no is probably the most obvious and important part of stepping away from being a people-pleaser, but saying no can be difficult. What I have found really helped me was to delay my response; instead of staying no straight away and perhaps feeling a little bit guilty, I would practise a line or two that allows me to take time and respond when I feel comfortable. When I am responding no, I remain empathetic in situations where I feel it, but I don't allow myself to feel guilty for saying no. I always acknowledge the other person's feelings or the stress they might be under, followed by my reasons as to why I can't do what they're asking. I used to follow a no with a long justification for doing so when the easiest way is just a short, simple, matter-of-fact 'no'.

These techniques and experiences I have shared are all things that I still have to remind myself to practise every day. I'm by no means a professional or where I want to be; I am still learning every day. It was really important to me that this book doesn't come across as preachy or didactic or 'Look at me – if I can do it, you can too!' I wanted to share my story with you in as raw and as truthful a way as I could, for many reasons. One of them was simply because of the support and positive reaction I have had over the years on my social media. I have made numerous friends and had some of the most intimate conversations of my life with people willing to open up to me, which will stay with me forever. I felt alone for so long, so having strangers share with me and lead me to opportunities that I never saw for myself has been immensely rewarding. Being so open and vulnerable on a social media platform has helped me heal in so many ways.

Taking back my power

To this day, I have triggers and flashbacks of moments I had long buried and forgotten. I have memories I will probably never share with anyone. I have shared more with you in this book than I have before because I don't think it would be a true representation of my full journey if I didn't. I didn't want to sugar-coat my story or lead people to believe that it's been an easy journey. From the beginning, I wanted to take my time and open up and share.

We all have a past, but our past does not define us; it teaches us lessons. We will always be faced with difficulties and bumps in the road, but when we work through them and come out the other side, it's always more fulfilling, even if it doesn't seem like it at the time.

WE ALL HAVE A PAST, BUT OUR PAST DOES NOT DEFINE US; IT TEACHES US LESSONS.

I remember queuing at 8 o'clock in the morning with a buggy and a suitcase to get a bed in a shelter, and not one person close to me had any idea that this was my life. I felt weak and like a failure, but when I look back on that day, I see strength and resilience in my showing up and doing what I could for Carter and me. I didn't see that at the time at all, but often we don't realise the things we are capable of in the moment.

Another moment that really sticks in my mind was just after Christmas 2016. I was sitting on my own on my sitting-room floor in London. I had probably sat crying for over an hour because of how low I felt.

I was exhausted from the constant anxiety, weak from the constant sadness and completely crippled with loneliness. I couldn't see as far as tomorrow. I had no idea if I would ever get home to my family and friends. I had almost accepted that this was going to be my future. I was riddled with guilt that I had already failed my son. I don't think I had an ounce of hope left in me. My life was in the worst place, and I couldn't see a way out. I honestly believed nothing was going to change. I know there are other people out there in similar situations who may never want to open up or talk about it. Still, I hope that my sharing the ups and downs of what I went through makes someone feel a little less lonely or provides a little comfort in knowing that it's not just you and that you're never alone. I didn't see a future for myself then, and I would never have imagined that I would get myself to where I am today. I know some circumstances feel impossible. But things can and do change, and nothing is permanent; this moment or this feeling will pass, and you are capable of changing just as much as anyone else out there.

I WOULD NEVER HAVE IMAGINED THAT I WOULD GET MYSELF TO WHERE I AM TODAY.

I wanted to be honest about my mindset throughout this journey because we are constantly being bombarded with messages about positive mindsets, self-love and body confidence – which is great to see and the direction we need to go in, but it's not always easy. People sometimes look at me and my journey and just assume that I am there. I don't think most of us are, but I hope we can all be more open about it and unafraid to say, 'Actually, I don't feel my best, but that's okay because I'm acknowledging it and working on it.'

When it comes to food and diet, it's impossible to tell anyone what to do, as we are all built differently. Some people want to track and weigh, some want to use intuitive eating, and some want to try weight-loss surgery. You must do what is right for you and, most importantly, what works for you! Finding the balance is key. Cook more meals from scratch, cook with your family, cook new recipes, batch cook, plan your meals, and cook meals you enjoy! And still go out and live your life. Make memories and enjoy being social when you're out. Don't deprive yourself; don't say no to things because you're afraid of the calories. You can have a great week full of nutritious meals and plenty of walking and exercising, and still enjoy a meal out and a few drinks.

Remember that small changes all add up to make big differences. There's no rush: just keep doing the work and the results will follow. You won't get to the end of your life and say, 'I wish I never ate that box of chocolates,' or 'I wish I had spent longer in the gym and burned more

calories,' or 'I wish I worked harder to get rid of my cellulite.' So, when you find yourself worrying about those things, remember that they're the least important things about you and your life. We are so much more than our bodies. It's great to be active and healthy but it's not okay if we think about it 24/7. I already regret that I spent so much of my life in my negative headspace, consumed by thoughts about my body. Imagine looking back at your life and that's one of the main things for you too. I think you'll regret that.

So, from today, take the power back and own who you are; not who anyone else thinks you are or should be, but who you are! We all have the power within us. Trust yourself and trust the next chapter in your life – because you're the one writing it!

u

COOK MORE MEALS FROM SCRATCH, COOK WITH YOUR FAMILY, COOK NEW RECIPES, BATCH COOK, PLAN YOUR MEALS, AND COOK MEALS YOU ENJOY!

u

CARTER AND ME ON OUR HOLIDAYS AT SPANISH POINT, COUNTY CLARE. AFTER A SWIM, WE SAT ON THE BEACH TALKING FOR ABOUT TWO HOURS. I WILL CHERISH THIS MEMORY FOR EVER.

Journey
Essentials

I wanted to include a section where I share a few of the things that I introduced or changed in my daily life that helped me in my approach to fitness and a healthier lifestyle – because, believe me, before I began I had absolutely no idea what I was doing! As I said earlier in the book, what works for one person won't always work for another, so make sure you do and find things that bring you joy. I speak a lot about the gym because that's what I love, but for you that might be swimming, hiking, dancing or skateboarding – who knows? And you'll never catch me talking about running because I find zero joy in it and will never be a runner!

Fail to plan, plan to fail

When I began my journey, I started simple and looked at the basics. I wanted to change my life after what felt like years of failed attempts. So, I stepped back and looked at what was making me give up each time and at what point. For me, it was the fear of failure that would stop me or hold me back.

> ## TAKE A MOMENT TO THINK ABOUT WHAT IT'S BEEN FOR YOU THAT HAS MADE YOU STOP

For this to work for me this time, I needed something that suited my lifestyle and would easily become a part of my everyday life. I dreaded that feeling of starting a new diet, when you almost feel as though you're preparing yourself to take on Mount Everest and your only two options are failure or success. Something I knew how to do well in other areas of my life was planning and organising, and so for the first 12 months of my journey, I really lived by the saying 'fail to plan, plan to fail'.

MY FOOD DIARY

I got myself a food diary and decided that I would plan my three meals per day for the next seven days. It made things easier for me when I knew exactly what I had planned for the day ahead. Here are my golden rules for planning my meals:

- I decided that this time around I was not going to be cutting out any food groups, or foods, for that matter. Previously when I started a 'diet' I would deny myself a lot of the foods I enjoyed, so no chocolate, no bread, no sweets, no butter, etc. This just isn't sustainable – well, it wasn't for me anyway! Who wants to never allow themselves to eat certain foods they love? And the fact that I knew I 'couldn't' have them only made me think about them a lot more than I normally would.

- I made sure that my approach matched up with my goals, not with what I saw other people doing. This time I wanted to change my lifestyle; I wanted a better understanding of nutrition and I wanted to improve my health. For the first time, I wasn't looking for a quick fix or to drop as much weight as possible. I wanted to implement changes that I could carry on with day to day, and I knew that restricting myself from certain foods wouldn't work.

- I still put chocolate into my plan most days, if not every day, after dinner. Planning this way really helped me cut out my habit of mindless eating. Grabbing some toast/crackers/biscuits here and there would all add up, but never satisfy me and I would more than likely forget that food had even passed my lips.

- I would try to make sure that at least one meal per week was a new one. I get bored easily and have never been one to have chicken, rice and broccoli five days a week. New meals allowed me to get that little bit creative in the kitchen and look forward to trying a new meal. This was around the time that my love for creating fakeaways began. If I had a craving for a certain food or takeaway, I would recreate it at home, just a healthier version. This is what worked for me – having the same meal every day of the week might work for you, but I knew I needed that creativity and freedom if I wanted to stick to my plan.

- When planning my 21 meals for the week, I would make sure that each meal was satisfying and nutritious. It made it easier to plan three filling meals and snacks that fit into my plan. It gave me structure when I needed it, and I would make sure the meals and snacks were enough so that I wouldn't be left feeling hungry.

- Every Sunday evening, I would take 20 minutes to sit down and plan for the week ahead. Try to pick a day and time that you know will work for you. If you regularly do the shopping on a Sunday

morning, it might be just after work on Friday evening or a Saturday morning. When I didn't take the time to plan my days, the food would usually end up being quick, convenient and not very nutritious. I made sure to prioritise those 20 minutes every Sunday for myself.

- Writing a shopping list always went hand-in-hand with my meal planning. In the beginning, I found it easier to do an online food shop (it helped me with temptation and impulsive buying). I would only get what I needed for our meals, and I always made sure that the fresh ingredients would be used in multiple meals. This way, I rarely had food waste, and it has worked in my favour budget-wise. Planning your weekly meals, especially for a busy family, is a great way to help with time management too. There's no standing around staring into the fridge and cupboards, looking for inspiration for what to cook. It can help with meal prepping, too; I would check tomorrow's dinner plan, grab what I needed and prepare what I could ahead of time to make it easier for myself.

- I would plan quick and easy meals or batch-cooked dinners from the freezer on the days I knew I would be busy. I would plan meals that required more prep and cooking time on the days I had more time.

- I recognise that there will be days when things don't go to plan, and that's fine.

Here's a sample of my food diary:

	BREAKFAST	LUNCH	DINNER
MONDAY	WARM APPLE AND CINNAMON PORRIDGE p123	PIZZA BAGEL p167	CREAMY MUSHROOM PEPPERED CHICKEN p191
TUESDAY	HIGH PROTEIN YOGHURT WITH BERRIES	JEN'S PROTEIN CAESAR BOWL p160	LOVELY LAYERED LASAGNE p184
WEDNESDAY	OVERNIGHT BISCUIT CAKE p131	SCRAMBLED EGGS WITH SALMON AND DILL p170	CURRY IN A HURRY p222
THURSDAY	SMOKED SALMON EGG MUFFINS p139	CREAMY GARLIC MUSHROOMS ON TOAST p151	FAKEAWAY FISH AND CHIPS p238
FRIDAY	JEN GOES NUTS FOR GRANOLA p127	OPEN TOASTIE p166	HONEY CHILLI CRISPY CHICKEN p211
SATURDAY	PECAN COFFEE SLICE p132	SPICY MAYO TUNA BOWL p163	EVERYONE'S FAVOURITE ENCHILADAS p176
SUNDAY	BACON AND CHEESE EGG TORTILLA p143	TOMATO AND BASIL SOUP p155	CHEESE-STUFFED SPICY MEATBALLS p183

I would simply do my best on those days and slip straight back into my plan. Out of 21 meals a week, if 5 of them were off-plan or didn't happen, I still had 16 planned meals. Then there were days when I just might not feel like the meal I had planned for myself, so I would switch it up and move meals around for the week.

THE 30-MINUTE RULE

I really believe that a lot of us think cooking meals from scratch involves too much time and effort, but it really doesn't have to. In the last couple of years, I have tried not to spend more than 30 minutes prepping and cooking. Working full-time and coming home to my young son in the evenings was tough enough, so the last thing I wanted to be doing was standing in the kitchen for longer than I needed.

I still wanted to cook meals that I enjoyed and would allow me to stay on my plan. I didn't over-complicate things, and I would keep it as simple as I could for myself. Using leftovers is a great way to get the most from your meals. I don't like having the same dinner two days in a row, so I would make simple changes to create a new meal.

If I had spaghetti Bolognese, for example, the leftovers would easily be turned into chilli; fajitas could be turned into a fajita bowl; pasta dishes can be easily turned into pasta salads; and a roast chicken could be tomorrow's chicken curry.

Dealing with cravings

I believe that if you are craving something, it's best not to deprive yourself all the time. No one wants to cut the things they enjoy out completely. Finding the balance between overindulging and enjoying things in moderation can be tough. Doing things like replacing a few of your takeaways with fakeaways will allow you to feed those cravings and still maintain that healthy balance.

From the beginning, I made sure that my plan worked for me and for what I enjoyed eating. Chocolate in the evening with a cup of tea when Carter was in bed was something I made sure to keep in! I also found it helpful to always have low-calorie snacks at home, both sweet and savoury. This gave me options when I was craving something in the evenings or between meals. Having an evening snack of high-protein yoghurt, berries and some crumbled biscuit or broken chocolate was a great one when I fancied something sweet. In the past, when I would diet, I'd always had the mindset of 'don't have it in the house and then you can't eat it'! But that would leave me thinking about what I wanted all night and would usually lead to a binge to satisfy a prolonged craving. There are so many options nowadays for sweet and savoury snacks. Some of the things I like to keep in my snack drawer are popcorn, crisps, cheese dippers, high-protein puddings, mini cookie bags and dark chocolate squares with peanut butter. I would often have oat cookies, homemade protein balls and banana and peanut butter bites dipped in chocolate to really satisfy a sweet craving!

I worked on recognising why I was craving something: was it out of boredom? Was I emotional? Was it my time of the month? Previously, I would eat out of boredom a lot, but I found that when I had my three planned meals and snacks, I wouldn't have that 'boredom hunger' quite so often.

u

TAKE A MOMENT TO THINK ABOUT WHAT THE LAST THING YOU CRAVED WAS AND WHY

u

Keeping active and busy was also a great way to avoid boredom. The more I sat around doing nothing and feeling lethargic, the more my mind would turn to food, and then my body would crave it for a quick spike of energy. You don't need to do anything big and drastic like spring-cleaning the house or running a marathon to get you up and busy. I always have a to-do list on my phone (I've always been a list person!), and items on it range from tiny things like sending an email to ordering a certain book online for Carter or fixing a shelf in my room. So now, if I

was at home with free time and found myself eating out of boredom, I would have a look at my list and tick a few things off.

Here are a few examples that have kept me busy in the past:

- Plan my meals or write a shopping list out

- Go for a short walk and listen to an uplifting podcast or music

- Call a friend for a catch-up

- Housework

- 30 minutes of reading

- Clear out my wardrobe

- Try out a new recipe

- Meal prep

- Some rare me time, including a pamper session

FAKEAWAYS

If you are craving certain foods, you can always recreate them at home. You'd be surprised at how easy this can be done – some of my favourite fakeaway recipes are the Nation's Favourite Spice Bag (p. 217), Curry in a Hurry (p. 222), Honey Chilli Crispy Chicken (p. 211), Loaded Taco Fries (p. 226) and Hot and Spicy Crispy Chicken Burger (p. 230). I make simple swaps such as using a spray oil rather than free pouring oil, cooking in the air fryer or oven rather than frying, using less-than-5-per-cent-fat mince, and even breading my own chicken and fish instead of buying more processed ones from the shops. When it comes to things like pasta sauces, it's so easy to make your own rather than using a jar – and you can make sure they're packed with veg and flavour. I love my condiments, especially garlic sauce, so I played around with the ingredients until I made a decent one (turn to p. 269 for the recipe!). Rather than using full-fat mayo and oils, I swap it for some natural yoghurt and lighter mayo.

Emotional eating

This is what I struggled with the most, and to this day, I can still find myself slipping back into this pattern from time to time. It's been a long, personal journey for me: learning how to recognise this behaviour in myself and learning the tools that work for me when I need them. When I really struggled with losing weight in the past, weight-loss surgery was always at the forefront of my mind. But every time I thought about doing it, my gut told me it was my mind that I needed to work on. I don't think weight-loss surgery would have worked for me, personally; it wouldn't have helped me with what I struggled with. I didn't want to rely on food anymore as

an emotional crutch. I wanted to educate myself on food as much as I could and invest in coaches who could work alongside me.

HOW I RECOGNISED THE CYCLE

With emotional eating, it was always the same cycle for me. When I was feeling stressed, overwhelmed, upset or angry, my mind would turn to food. I would think of nothing else, only the foods I wanted to binge on. I would try and physically push those feelings down by shoving as much food into me as possible. I would binge until I felt uncomfortable, and then, within minutes, I would be left feeling guilty and powerless over food – on top of the emotions I was feeling before I binged. In the moments before I ate, I convinced myself that I was in control and would just have a little. But as soon as I took that first bite, I would lose all control. Sometimes I wouldn't even remember what I had eaten – I was simply putting as much of it as I could into me.

TAKE A MOMENT

When I felt that intense 'hunger' overcome me, it was hugely helpful to take a moment to recognise how I was truly feeling. There are a number of steps that I found useful to walk through:

* I would ask myself: when did I last eat?

ME AND CARTER AND MY DAD IN 2018.

- I would think about the kinds of foods I was craving. Then I'd ask myself: will this food make me feel better about myself 10 minutes from now?

- Next question: will it solve the situation that is causing me to want to eat? I would always take a few minutes to see if the urge would pass, because it is often short-lived.

- If I was still obsessing over a certain food at this point, I'd try to physically remove myself from the situation when possible. I'd distract my mind by going for a short walk or even getting some housework done (not for everyone, I know!).

- When I was first trying to break my emotional eating cycle, I would sometimes go to the kitchen when the urge came over me and pick up the food I wanted. I would hold it in my hand and weigh up whether this was really what I wanted.

- If I was in a low place or feeling very upset, having someone to talk or vent to always made me feel much better, even if it was just a text. I found it hard to do this for a long time because of the guard I had built up, but friends will always want to listen and help when they can. After talking to someone, the urge to binge has usually passed for me. Alternatively, some people find it helpful to journal. Expressing how you're feeling at the time by writing it all out can often lift the weight of it off you.

SAVOUR IT

If none of the above worked, then I was likely just hungry, and I would, of course, eat. But rather than stuffing it into me, I'd take five minutes to sit down and enjoy whatever I was eating (and just make sure not to eat seven of them!).

MY WHYS

When I was a little further into recognising my emotional eating, I worked on a new tool I would call my whys. By this point in my weight-loss journey, I was beginning to set myself small goals and intentions that I wanted to achieve. These could have been something as simple as going for a bike ride with Carter or adding an extra five minutes to my walking route. Any time I felt the urge to binge, I would remind myself of the reasons why I didn't want to be doing it: all my whys that I was excited to achieve. I would remind myself of all the things I wanted that were important to me – more important than binging. Crucially, my whys changed all the time because as I went through my journey, I grew, and the things that were important to me changed also. So my whys were always relevant to me at that particular time. I would focus on my whys and the things I wanted more than the five minutes of satisfaction I would get from a binge.

A guide for gym newbies

Becoming more active in general had a hugely positive effect on my life. From the day I set foot in my gym, Back2Basics, in 2017 up until today, that space has been a massive part of my journey – not only in relation to weight loss and training but also in terms of helping me grow into myself in many areas. I have confidence that I am capable of achieving things that I never had before. Since training there, my mindset, my drive and my self-belief have all skyrocketed from where I once was. I wasn't just becoming physically stronger in the gym; I was also becoming mentally

stronger than I had ever been. I was lucky enough to find a space that was full of like-minded people who are now some of my closest friends, as well as some of the best coaches around, who are constantly learning and evolving alongside us.

ME AND MOE WORKING ON MY TECHNIQUE!

Investing your time and money in a quality trainer is one of the best things you can do for yourself. It's an investment in yourself and your health. Setting aside that hour a few times a week is something we all deserve to give ourselves. From the beginning of my journey, I never allowed myself to feel guilty as a parent for taking that time for me. I know it's easy to feel selfish when you're taking time to do things for yourself, but I was working to better myself, and that helped me to become the best parent I could be.

Joining a new gym can be a scary thought for a lot of people, and for me, it was amplified in my head because of my size.

My very brief experience in previous gyms had not been the most positive. I imagined myself in the gym in such a negative way before I had even joined, thinking, *It's the one place you don't expect to see fat people, Jen, so you'll definitely stand out.* I was already making up my mind that gyms weren't for me before even trying. But when I joined Back2Basics, it was different for me: I wanted to train to get stronger and fitter, and I wanted my own little escape from my mind at the time. I wasn't looking to go so that I could lose weight or 'get skinny'.

FINDING THE RIGHT ONE

When I was looking to join a gym in 2017, one of the most important things for me was a safe and comfortable environment. That was the first thing I felt with Seán at Back2Basics on my very first day. I never once felt an ounce of judgement, a funny look or an unwanted opinion. His attitude was literally, 'Okay, let's see what you can do, and we're gonna work together from there.'

The location of your gym is also important as you want to make sure it's somewhere that is convenient for you. If it's an hour's drive or two bus rides away, the chances are that you'll slowly feel less inclined to go regularly.

WHAT TO WEAR?

I worried a lot about what to wear to the gym – which may sound silly, but at the time, I really didn't have many options. I was self-conscious about every single part of my body and would want it all completely covered up. But I wasn't going to let that stop me from going, so I went online to a men's plus-size shop and ordered myself some long-sleeved black cotton tops to go with my black cotton leggings. The material was so thick and horrible to wear in a gym session, but I didn't care because it made me feel more comfortable knowing that everything was covered up. It took me a long time to realise that nobody is looking at what you're wearing in the gym. We all show up with the same intention for ourselves. We don't go to see what people are wearing. So wear whatever you feel comfortable in.

GET A GYM BUDDY

It's always nice if you have a friend to go with. In the beginning, it really helped me to have Grace by my side as support; we would always encourage each other when we needed it. Or, if you're going on your own, that's a good way to break down barriers and meet new people. And, of course, it can also simply just be you – your escape for some me-time.

RESIST COMPARISON

Never ever compare yourself to anyone else in the gym. We are all built completely differently, and we all work at our own pace. Comparing yourself to the person next to you is pointless; they could have been training five days a week for the last five years. You are not there to reach their level of fitness or achieve their goals. You are there to push yourself, work on your own level of fitness and achieve your own goals. If you stay consistent with your training, you can always look back on your own progress and compare against your past self.

Walking into the gym for the first time can often be the hardest part. I know that, for me, I felt like every single person was looking at me and judging me. But they're not. Everyone there is too focused on themselves and on getting through their workout. They will most likely have their own insecurities as well and could be thinking or worrying the same way you are. Starting in the gym could be the beginning of a new journey or a newfound love of fitness for you, like it was for me. Don't let worry hold you back or be the reason that you don't invest in yourself. Find yourself a great trainer that you trust and take it slow. This may be a whole new world and routine for you and your body – so listen to your body! And, most importantly, enjoy the process.

Building habits

Sitting down every week to plan for the week ahead was one of the most important parts of my journey. Habits are so important – they are small achievements that we can build on without even realising it. Here are some of the small habits I gently let go of or picked up.

WATER

I really did start with the basics when building habits – something as small as how much water I was having throughout the day. In the past, I would easily have got through plenty of days where I only had one glass of water, or even days where the only water I had was from my Americanos. To make drinking more water a habit, I made sure that I had one pint with each of my three meals. This was an easy way to not forget, and then after a week or so I upped it to five pints a day – until eventually it becomes so part of your routine that you don't even think about it. The more water I drank throughout the day, the better I felt, and I really noticed the benefits in my skin too, which was a nice bonus. Hydration is key!

WALKING

My steps have been a huge part of my journey and have helped me massively, both physically and mentally. Before I began my journey, I absolutely hated walking anywhere and would find an excuse to avoid it almost always. Walking for too long was very uncomfortable for me, and I would be embarrassed at how quickly I would get out of breath or struggle. When I began to introduce

ON A NIGHT AWAY WITH THE GIRLS IN 2022.

IN CAPPADOCIA, TURKEY, IN 2022. SERVING MY BEST 'ACT NATURAL' POSE!

walking more at the start of my journey, I took it slow, starting with even walking around my estate for 15 to 20 minutes on my own in the evenings. After a few weeks, when I could manage that with no struggle, I would increase the length or time of the walk. I began to look forward to getting out in the evenings after Carter was in bed to clear my head. I then started to walk to work to increase my steps and continued walking in the evening with friends. I love doing the school run (walk!) with Carter because it's only 10 minutes and it's a nice way for us both to start our day and have the chats (he's seven now, so I'm sure I won't have this for much longer).

GYM TIME

As I said before, the gym may not be for you – but whatever your physical activity is, it can be hard to build that habit and stay consistent. When I first began in the gym, I attended personal training twice a week, which I gradually increased to three and then eventually five times a week. I still go five times a week because I enjoy that one hour in the morning totally for myself, and it makes me feel better for the rest of the day. There's no point in forcing yourself to attend something you don't enjoy, so make sure you look forward to your exercise and don't overdo it to the point where you make yourself sick of it! As soon as my alarm goes off, I don't even think about it; I just get up and go because I know how great I'll feel in an hour's time – I have yet to regret a workout that I got

up for! I know that with busy schedules, family and work, it can be hard to fit exercise in, and I know that when Carter was younger I would sometimes feel guilty leaving him. So, I made a plan that worked for me: I would get up two hours earlier and go to my class before he was awake, and I would never train on Saturday or Sunday because that's our time.

SELF-TALK

This was, and still is, definitely the hardest one for me. Most people will tell me to look in the mirror and repeat positive affirmations to myself; I even encourage Carter to do this from time to time. But I won't lie: I often feel silly and uncomfortable doing this. The more you do it, however, the easier it gets – and you will believe what you're hearing yourself say. For this kind of exercise, I prefer to journal. If I catch myself talking or thinking negatively about myself, I will document it in writing. I'll ask myself, 'Why am I saying this about myself? Is there any truth to what I am saying? Would I say this to a friend? Am I helping or hurting myself? How can I turn this negative thought into a positive one?' I don't beat myself up when I catch myself doing it; I just recognise it, acknowledge it and do my best to stop it each time.

u

TRY TO THINK OF A FEW SMALL, POSITIVE CHANGES YOU CAN MAKE THIS WEEK. HOW CAN YOU BUILD ON THEM IN A MONTH? IN A YEAR?

u

LIFESTYLE > DIET

The most important word you should replace on your journey is swapping the word 'diet' for the word 'lifestyle'. This is about finding a way that you can live your life to the fullest while still maintaining a healthy, happy lifestyle. There will always be times when things are out of your control, which might feel like failures or setbacks. But that's life – it will never be plain sailing and there will always be a spanner thrown in the works somewhere. Trying to stay motivated during these times can be hard; it's not something we can just switch on and off. Having trust in yourself and knowing what you are capable of is one thing that I worked on. Normally, self-doubt would be my first way of thinking and it is hard to stop that creeping in, but we all have the strength within us. We just need to dig deep and trust ourselves.

Coming home from holidays, or after holiday seasons when we are off-plan for a long period of time, is when a lot of us struggle. Going from eating what you want back into a routine or structure can be difficult to adjust to. When I go off-plan for a long period of time, I gain big – that's just how my body works. I have gone on a week's holiday before and come home almost 20 lbs up. What always worked for me was to get straight back into my routine, and to be honest, after indulging for a long period, I would almost be looking forward to some normality and structure. But I know that for a lot of people, when they see that number on the scales go up, they get the urge to throw in the towel. It almost feels as though all your hard work and effort have been undone in such a short time.

But that's not the case. The weight gain could be down to several things: menstrual cycle, how you're sleeping, too much salt in your foods, water retention, levels of activity and so on. When your body adjusts back to its normal routine, the rest will follow. After a holiday, my appetite is normally bigger because I would have been eating more than usual, so I make sure that I'm filling up on high-protein and really nutritious foods. I also increase my water intake and try my best to catch up on as much sleep as possible. All these things help our bodies recover from an indulgent period, and within a few days, I always feel much better in myself and have a lot more energy than I would have if I just continued indulging after my holiday.

ME AND CARTER IN SAN JUAN.

Knowing this has made it easier for me not to dread going 'off-plan' when I would previously have worried about the 'damage' I would be doing. Instead, I now really appreciate the off-plan periods because I know I have my routine to fall back into. This removes the guilty feeling that I would get. My life isn't about 'starving' myself 90 per cent of the time to earn extra calories and go wild off-plan; it's about knowing that I've found a balance that works for me and enables me to live a strong, healthy lifestyle 100 per cent of the time. A diet can often be a temporary fix, but a lifestyle is a permanent, sustainable change.

My Recipes

Breakfast, as we all know, is the most important meal of the day. I never had a huge appetite in the morning – I still don't – but I make sure I fuel myself with something no matter how busy I am. Spending five minutes on breakfast prep the night before makes my life so much easier on busy mornings.

Breakfasts

Warm Apple and Cinnamon Porridge

340 KCAL **10.5g** PROTEIN

Porridge is always a great go-to breakfast to keep you fuelled. It doesn't have to be boring, either – you can mix in whatever you fancy to bulk it up. I love adding different fruits, depending on the time of year; and when I'm training it's handy to throw in a scoop of protein powder.

40g **porridge oats**

200ml **hazelnut milk**

1½ tsp **cinnamon**

1 **apple** (half grated and half thinly sliced)

1 tsp **sweetener** (I use stevia leaf)

2 tbsp **fat-free Greek yoghurt**

75g **blueberries**

1. Put the oats, milk, cinnamon and grated apple in a saucepan.

2. Bring the mixture to the boil and then quickly reduce the heat to low. Stir continuously for 5 minutes until it reaches a thick consistency.

3. Take the saucepan off the heat and add the sweetener and the Greek yoghurt for extra creaminess.

4. Scatter over the sliced apple, a handful of blueberries and some extra cinnamon to decorate.

TIP

If you have time the night before, leave the porridge oats soaking in the milk, grated apple and cinnamon overnight. It makes it so much creamier.

Swiss Roll Pancake

SERVES 1

446
KCAL

31.5g
PROTEIN

This has been a favourite of mine since the beginning of my journey. It is really filling and could easily make a lighter breakfast for two people. It is a delicious way of getting lots of protein to start your day. I love making these for everyone at the weekend. You can add nut butters, fruit or chocolate spreads – whatever you fancy!

40g **porridge oats**

1 **egg**, beaten

100g **fat-free Greek yoghurt**

1 tsp **cocoa powder**

pinch of **baking powder**

100g **vanilla-flavoured quark** or **protein yoghurt** (I use Aldi 25g protein vanilla yoghurt)

2 tbsp **reduced-sugar strawberry jam**

100g **strawberries**, chopped

1. In a blender, whizz the oats to a flour-like consistency.

2. Add the egg, yoghurt, cocoa powder and baking powder and blend into a smooth batter.

3. Pour the batter into a non-stick pan over a medium heat to make one large, thick pancake.

4. When you see small holes appear in the top it is ready to flip over and cook the other side.

5. Lay the pancake on a plate, spread the vanilla quark all over it and then add the jam on top.

6. Scatter some chopped strawberries over the jam. I like to roll up the pancake and slice it like a swiss roll!

TIP

I roll it up nice and tight, so I don't add too many strawberries. Hold the pancake closed with one hand and use your other hand to slice it.

JEN'S FAVOURITE

Jen Goes Nuts for Granola

20 PORTIONS

127
KCAL

2.7g
PROTEIN

PER PORTION

This recipe is so convenient and delicious. You can change the nuts to suit your palate and maybe add in some dried fruit too. I love a crunchy granola and it's perfect for sprinkling over a bowl of yoghurt or porridge.

4 tbsp **olive oil**

4 tbsp **honey**

1 tsp **sea salt**

1 tsp **cinnamon**

splash of **vanilla extract**

260g **porridge oats**

7 tbsp **walnuts**

7 tbsp **hazelnuts**

3 tbsp **flaked almonds**

2 tbsp **chia seeds**

50g **raisins** or **dried berries** (optional)

1. Preheat the oven to 150°C/130°C fan/gas mark 2.

2. Put the oil, honey, salt, cinnamon and vanilla in a large bowl and mix well.

3. Add the oats, nuts (you can crush them a little if you like) and seeds.

4. Line a large baking tray with greaseproof paper and use a spatula to spread the mixture evenly on it.

5. Pop it in the oven for 30 minutes. Halfway through cooking, take out the tray and stir everything around so that it all gets cooked evenly.

6. Remove from the oven and allow to cool. When it's cooled, add the raisins or dried berries, if using.

7. Store in an airtight container or jar. It should last up to eight weeks.

Oat Cookie Combo Platter

MAKES 6
CHOCOLATE COOKIES

93 KCAL   **2g** PROTEIN

MAKES 6
CINNAMON AND RAISIN COOKIES

76 KCAL   **1.7g** PROTEIN

These are so handy for breakfast on the go or for kids' lunchboxes. You really only need bananas and oats for the basic recipe, but you can add in anything you like. Carter and I always split the cookies into white and milk chocolate ones for him and raisin and cinnamon ones for me, with some honey added for sweetness and chewiness. He is not a fan of raisins in his cookies!

2 ripe **bananas**

150g **porridge oats**

2 tbsp **honey**

3 tbsp **chocolate chips**

3 tbsp **raisins**

1 tbsp **cinnamon**

1. Preheat the oven to 190°C/170°C fan/gas mark 5.

2. In a bowl, mash the bananas thoroughly and then stir in the oats, honey and any extra ingredients you like, such as nuts, seeds, peanut butter or shredded coconut.

3. Put half the mixture into another bowl. Add the chocolate chips to one bowl and the raisins and cinnamon to the other and mix each well.

4. Spoon tablespoons of the dough onto a layer of greaseproof paper on a baking tray. A heaped tablespoon will make one cookie.

5. Pop into the oven and bake for 15–20 minutes, turning the cookies over halfway through.

Overnight Biscuit Cake

SERVES 1

372 KCAL · **31g** PROTEIN

Who doesn't love cake for breakfast? This is one of those breakfasts that tastes too good to be true. You can make it with no toppings and just use the wheat biscuits, milk and quark/yoghurt or you can indulge yourself and get creative with the toppings. Lemon cheesecake, chocolate, different berries ... the options are endless!

1 **Weetabix**

80ml **low-fat milk**

50g fresh **raspberries**, plus a handful to garnish

200g pot **raspberry-flavoured quark** or **protein yoghurt**

1 tbsp **white chocolate**, roughly chopped

1 tbsp **reduced-sugar raspberry jam** (optional)

1. In a small, flat-bottomed container, crush the Weetabix until flaky. Add the milk and mix to combine. Then, using the back of a spoon, press the mixture down firmly until the surface is smooth.

2. Mix the fresh raspberries into the raspberry-flavoured quark or yoghurt and spread on top of the wheat biscuit base.

3. Top with some more fresh raspberries, chopped white chocolate and a drizzle of raspberry jam, if using. Leave to set in the fridge overnight for a delicious breakfast.

JEN'S FAVOURITE

Pecan Coffee Slice

MAKES 6 SLICES

160
KCAL

7.5g
PROTEIN

PER SLICE

This is a great recipe for the whole family to enjoy or a perfect one for batch cooking so that your breakfast is ready to go for the week ahead. The slices make a delicious snack with a cup of tea or coffee. They're so easy to make, and you can throw in whatever flavours you like. They will keep in an airtight container in the fridge for up to five days.

1 medium-sized very ripe **banana**

120g **porridge oats**

2 **eggs**, beaten

200g **fat-free Greek yoghurt**

2 tsp **baking powder**

2 tsp **instant coffee**

8 tbsp **pecans**

1–2 tbsp **sweetener**, according to taste

vanilla yoghurt or **cream**, to serve

1. Preheat the oven to 190°C/170°C fan/gas mark 5.

2. Mash the banana with a fork, then add all the other ingredients (except the vanilla yoghurt or cream) and mix together.

3. Line an oven dish (17 x 27 cm) with baking paper.

4. Spoon the mixture into the oven dish and cook for 40 minutes in the centre of the oven.

5. Once cooled, cut into 6 slices.

6. This is lovely served with some vanilla yoghurt or cream.

Strawberry and Banana Loaf

141
KCAL

6.5g
PROTEIN

PER SLICE

This loaf is ideal for a sharing breakfast straight out of the oven or for keeping in the fridge as a go-to snack. I love a slice of it with some jam and berries.

1 very ripe **banana**

120g **porridge oats**

2 **egg whites**

200g **fat-free Greek yoghurt**

1 tbsp **sweetener**

150g **strawberries**, chopped

low-calorie spray cooking oil

1 tbsp **pumpkin seeds**

4 or 5 **strawberries**, to garnish

1. Preheat the oven to 190°C/170°C fan/gas mark 5.

2. In a mixing bowl, mash the banana with a fork, and then add in the oats, egg whites, yoghurt and sweetener and mix really well.

3. Add the chopped strawberries and mix to combine.

4. Spray a 450g (1lb) loaf tin with cooking spray. Pour the mixture into the loaf tin.

5. Halve the whole strawberries and pop them on top. Scatter over the pumpkin seeds.

6. Bake on the middle rack of the oven for 40–45 minutes.

7. Remove from the oven and allow to cool.

Protein Pancakes

SERVES 1

365 KCAL · **33g** PROTEIN

This is one of my favourite breakfasts after the gym – it's so filling and packed with protein. I sometimes add protein powder if I want to get some extra protein in. You could top the pancakes with some syrup, peanut butter or chocolate spread and a side of yoghurt. It's almost like having cake for breakfast!

40g **porridge oats**
1 **egg white**
100g **fat-free Greek yoghurt**
pinch of **baking powder**
100g **blueberries**
low-calorie **spray cooking oil**
100g **vanilla-flavoured quark** or **protein yoghurt**

1. Blitz the oats to a flour-like consistency in a blender. Add the egg white, Greek yoghurt and a pinch of baking powder and blend again.

2. Once blended, add half the blueberries to the batter.

3. Spray a pan with oil and pour a ladle of the mixture onto the pan on a medium heat. Depending on how thick you like them, you will get three or four pancakes from the mixture.

4. Once you see bubbles appear on the pancake, it is ready to flip over. They should be a nice golden-brown colour.

5. I like to stack them up, spreading vanilla quark and scattering blueberries between the layers.

Smoked Salmon Egg Muffins

85
KCAL

9.5g
PROTEIN

PER MUFFIN

I have made this dish from the beginning of my journey. These muffins are just so convenient, and you can make them as plain or as fancy as you like. They're lovely hot or cold, too, which makes them great for breakfasts or lunches on the go. I often pack mine with cheese and chicken or ham instead of smoked salmon for maximum protein.

4 **eggs**

½ tsp **cracked black pepper**, plus a little extra to garnish

1 tsp **fresh dill**, finely chopped, plus extra to garnish

low-calorie spray cooking oil

100g **smoked salmon**, sliced

handful **spinach leaves**, torn

1 **scallion**, finely chopped

60g **light cream cheese** (I use Philadelphia Lightest)

1. Preheat the oven to 190°C/170°C fan/gas mark 5.

2. Beat the eggs in a bowl with the cracked black pepper and dill.

3. Spray a muffin tin with some spray oil and spoon an equal amount of salmon, spinach and scallion into each.

4. Pour the egg mixture into each case until it's three-quarters full. Add a small dollop of cream cheese.

5. Pop in the oven for 20 minutes.

6. Remove from the oven and garnish with extra dill and pepper.

TIP

You can change these every time you make them and add whatever filling you like. Another great way to enjoy them is by lining the muffin cases or tin with ham slices before you start filling them.

Sundried Tomato, Pesto and Cheddar Egg Muffins

MAKES 6 LARGE MUFFINS

168 KCAL **12g** PROTEIN

PER MUFFIN

These are also great for lunches and snacks. They're perfect in the summer when I don't fancy a heavy dinner, or we're having picky bits in the garden. They go beautifully with salads, and a couple of these muffins are quite filling too – lots of protein!

4 eggs

200ml **low-fat milk**

salt and **pepper**

low-calorie spray cooking oil

40g **light Cheddar cheese**, grated

50g **sundried tomatoes**, chopped

2 tbsp **pesto** (see recipe on page 193)

basil leaves, to garnish (optional)

1. Preheat the oven to 190°C/170°C fan/gas mark 5.

2. Whisk the eggs and milk with salt and pepper to taste.

3. Spray a six-hole muffin tin with some spray oil and spoon an equal amount of grated cheese and sundried tomatoes into each.

4. Pour the egg and milk mixture over the sundried tomatoes and cheese, then top with a teaspoon of pesto.

5. Place in the oven for 25 minutes until the eggs are cooked through.

6. Remove from the oven and garnish with a few basil leaves, if you like.

Bacon and Cheese Egg Tortilla

SERVES 1

480
KCAL

38g
PROTEIN

This is a perfect weekend breakfast or brunch idea. It's so versatile and you can use different ingredients each time you make it. To spice it up, you could add some salsa and avocado. This will keep you full for ages and is packed with flavour and nutrition.

low-calorie spray cooking oil

2 **bacon medallions**

2 **eggs**, beaten

handful **spinach**, chopped

1 **tortilla wrap**

30g **light Cheddar cheese**, grated

1. Spray a frying pan with oil and cook the bacon for ten minutes over a low–medium heat. Remove the cooked bacon and set aside.

2. Pour the beaten eggs into the same pan over a medium heat and add the chopped spinach.

3. Once the egg is firm on the bottom but not set on top, place your wrap on it. The uncooked egg will stick to the wrap. Use a spatula all around the edge to lift it away from the pan, and flip to crisp the wrap side.

4. Spread the cheese all over the egg side and add the bacon on top.

5. Remove from the pan, fold it over and enjoy!

I find lunch can be the trickiest of our three meals, but once you plan it and set aside a small amount of time, you're good! When I'm at home for lunch I can be a little more creative and cook something nice in a short space of time. I have a bigger appetite at midday than I do first thing in the morning, so I have a much bigger lunch and smaller breakfast. For work and on-the-go lunches, I find the best approach for me is using leftovers from dinner the night before and meal-prepping at the start of the week.

Lunches

Scotch Eggs

240 KCAL   **30g** PROTEIN

PER SCOTCH EGG

These are really filling and can be eaten cold, so they're perfect for lunchboxes.

2 slices **bread**

1 tsp **paprika**

1 tsp **onion granules**

½ tsp **cayenne pepper**

500g **lean pork mince**

1 **onion**, diced

handful **fresh parsley**

1 tsp **garlic powder**

salt and **pepper**

6 **eggs**

low-calorie spray cooking oil

1. Preheat the oven to 180°C/160°C fan/gas mark 4. If using an air fryer, preheat it (for about 3 minutes) to 180°C.

2. Using a food processor, blend the bread, paprika, onion granules and cayenne pepper into fine crumbs and spread the crumbs out on a large plate.

3. Then blend the mince, onion, parsley, garlic powder, salt and pepper until smooth.

4. Beat one egg and set aside.

5. Place the other eggs in a saucepan and cover with cold water. Bring to the boil, then reduce the heat to a gentle simmer for 3–5 minutes, depending on how well you like your eggs cooked.

6. Transfer the eggs to a bowl of cold water, let them sit for a couple of minutes, then peel.

7. Wrap the mince mixture around each egg, dip into the beaten egg, and then coat in the breadcrumbs.

8. Spray each coated egg with spray oil and pop them into the oven or air fryer for 20 minutes.

TIP

To peel the eggs, I put them on a flat surface and use the palm of my hand to gently roll them back and forth until cracked all the way around. The colder the water is when you transfer them, the easier they peel – iced water works best.

Egg Calzone

SERVES 1

510 KCAL | **61g** PROTEIN

Egg wraps are a go-to lunch for me at the weekend, but sometimes I like to turn them into a calzone filled with spicy chicken and cheese. They are so filling they could easily be a dinner too, and they're packed with protein. It's a great way to make a few eggs a lot more egg-citing!

low-calorie spray cooking oil

1 skinless chicken breast, diced

3 medium-sized mushrooms, sliced

1 scallion, chopped

3 eggs, beaten with a splash of milk

100ml passata

½ tsp paprika

½ tsp garlic granules

salt and pepper

40g light Cheddar cheese, grated

30g light mozzarella, sliced

½ tsp chilli flakes

1. Preheat the oven to 190°C/170°C fan/gas mark 5.

2. Spray a pan with oil and lightly fry the diced chicken breast for 5 minutes until golden brown. Add the sliced mushrooms and chopped scallion.

3. While the chicken is cooking, pour the egg mixture into a different non-stick pan over a medium heat. Once the egg wrap is firm, use a spatula to flip it over and cook the other side, or place the pan under a medium grill to cook the top.

4. Once the chicken is cooked, add two-thirds of the passata, along with the paprika, garlic granules, salt and pepper, and stir.

5. Lay the cooked egg wrap on a baking tray covered with baking paper. Put the chicken mix on one half of the egg wrap and add half the grated Cheddar on top. Fold the other half of the egg wrap over the filled side.

6. Spread the remaining passata on top of the egg wrap, then add the rest of the grated Cheddar, sliced mozzarella and a sprinkle of chilli flakes.

7. Place in the oven for 10–15 minutes until the cheese is completely melted.

Stuffed Mushrooms

SERVES 1

206
KCAL

15.5g
PROTEIN

This is a lovely light lunch that's full of flavour. You can add in different ingredients, like bacon, breadcrumbs, spinach and cheese. The mushrooms are quite filling and very low in calories. A really handy one to throw in the air fryer too. I line my air fryer with some baking paper and place the mushrooms on it (which saves mess and cleaning up).

3 tbsp **light cream cheese**

1 **garlic clove**, crushed

1 **scallion** or **shallot**, finely chopped

1 tsp **chilli flakes**

1 tsp **dried chives**

2 **Portobello mushrooms**

cracked black pepper

1 tbsp **Parmesan**, grated

handful rocket leaves

1 tbsp **balsamic vinegar**

1. Preheat the oven to 190°C/170°C fan/gas mark 5. If using an air fryer, preheat it (for about 3 minutes) to 190°C.

2. Mix the cream cheese, garlic, scallion or shallot, chilli flakes and chives in a bowl.

3. Place the mushrooms on a baking tray, stem side up.

4. Spoon the cream cheese mixture into the mushrooms and top with some cracked black pepper and a sprinkle of Parmesan.

5. Cook in the oven or air fryer for 15–20 minutes.

6. Serve with rocket drizzled with balsamic vinegar.

Creamy Garlic Mushrooms on Toast

SERVES 1

260 KCAL   **16g** PROTEIN

Creamy mushrooms on toast is a real love-it-or-leave-it kind of meal, but I love it. It's so easy to throw together for a quick lunch. The light cream cheese makes it taste deliciously creamy and indulgent; and the calorie count is surprisingly low.

low-calorie spray cooking oil

8 **white mushrooms**, sliced

1 **garlic clove**, crushed

handful **spinach leaves**

pinch of **sea salt**

1 tbsp **light cream cheese**

1 tsp **black pepper**

1 tsp **dried parsley**

1 **ciabatta**, sliced

1. Spray a frying pan with some oil, add the mushrooms and garlic and cook over a low heat for 10 minutes until tender and lightly browned. Throw in most of the spinach with the sea salt, and let the spinach wilt – it should only take 2 or 3 minutes.

2. Take the pan off the heat and stir in the cream cheese along with the black pepper and dried parsley.

3. Pop the ciabatta slices in the toaster.

4. Lay the remaining spinach leaves on your toasted ciabatta and top with the creamy mushroom mixture.

JEN'S FAVOURITE

Mushroom Soup

63
KCAL

7g
PROTEIN

PER PORTION

Mushroom soup is easily one of my favourites, and this recipe is too easy not to try. It is packed with flavour and tastes really creamy – without using any cream!

low-calorie spray cooking oil

2 **onions**, finely chopped

1 **garlic clove**, finely chopped

600g **mushrooms**, sliced

2 **chicken stock cubes**, dissolved in 1 litre of **water**

1 tbsp **dried tarragon**

sea salt to taste

200g **fat-free fromage frais**

cracked black pepper

a few **chives**, chopped, to garnish

1. Heat a large saucepan and add some spray oil. Sweat off the onions over a gentle heat until they are translucent.

2. Add the garlic and mushrooms, and sweat them for about 15 minutes. Cooking them over a low heat and not allowing them to brown helps draw out their flavour.

3. Add the chicken stock, tarragon and sea salt, bring to the boil, then reduce the heat and simmer for 20 minutes.

4. Leave the soup to cool completely and then blend it until smooth.

5. Serve with a dollop of fromage frais, plenty of cracked black pepper and chives.

Tomato and Basil Soup

SERVES 6

120 KCAL · **5.5g** PROTEIN

PER PORTION

Of all the soups I make, this one is probably my favourite. It takes a little longer, as roasting the tomatoes slowly gives the best flavour. But the extra time is so worth it – it always goes down so well with everyone.

low-calorie spray cooking oil

750g **plum tomatoes**

a few pinches of **dried thyme**

a few pinches of **dried oregano**

2 **onions**, chopped

3 **garlic cloves**, chopped

400g **tin tomatoes**

2 tbsp **Worcestershire sauce**

1 **vegetable stock cube**

25g **fresh basil**

salt and **pepper**

1. Preheat the oven to 200°C/180°C fan/gas mark 6.

2. Line a baking tray with baking paper, spray with oil and spread the plum tomatoes on the tray in an even layer. Spray them with oil and sprinkle with salt, thyme and oregano.

3. Cook in the middle of the oven for 45–50 minutes until the tomato skins are soft, slightly browned in places and beginning to burst.

4. In a large pot over a medium heat, soften the chopped onions in some spray oil for 5 minutes and then add the chopped garlic. Cook on a medium heat for about 5 minutes until soft.

5. Add the tinned tomatoes, a little more oregano and thyme, the Worcestershire sauce, the vegetable stock cube and 1 litre of water. Stir in the fresh basil, bring to the boil and simmer for 30 minutes.

6. Take off the heat and add the roasted tomatoes, juices and all. Allow to cool completely and then blend until smooth.

TIP

If you prefer a creamier soup, you can add 200g of cottage cheese before blending.

JEN'S FAVOURITE

French Onion Soup

160
KCAL

7g
PROTEIN

PER PORTION

French onion soup always sounded fancy to me and too much effort to make at home, but it is surprisingly simple and requires very few ingredients. It's a lovely soup in both winter and summer and it's not too heavy.

25g **butter**

8 **onions**, peeled and cut into wedges

3 **garlic cloves**, finely chopped

3 tbsp **brown sugar** or 1 tbsp **sweetener**

2 **beef Oxo cubes**

1 tbsp fresh **thyme leaves**

salt and **pepper**, to taste

1 ball **light mozzarella**, sliced, to garnish

1. Melt the butter in a large pot over a medium heat, then add the onions and garlic and cook over a high heat, stirring constantly, for 5 minutes, making sure the onions don't burn. Reduce the heat to medium and continue cooking, stirring constantly, for a further 5 minutes.

2. Once the onions are soft, add the sweetener or sugar and stir again to make sure they are fully coated in the butter and sugar.

3. Put the lid on the saucepan and cook on a medium-high heat for about 15 minutes or until they begin to caramelise in the sugar and turn a light brown.

4. Now add the stock cubes, thyme, salt, pepper and 1 litre of water.

5. Bring to the boil, then reduce to a simmer and cook gently for 30 minutes.

6. This soup is served chunky, so ladle it into bowls and serve with mozzarella.

TIP

I like to use Oxo cubes specifically for this recipe as I find they have the strongest flavour.

Roast Butternut Squash and Red Pepper Soup

SERVES 6

71 KCAL   **2.2g** PROTEIN

PER PORTION

This is one of my favourite soups to make, especially in the autumn. I add chilli for a little kick to complement the sweetness of the roast squash.

1 **butternut squash**, halved and deseeded

2 **red bell peppers**, halved and deseeded

3 **onions** (1 halved, 2 chopped)

5 **garlic cloves**, peeled

low-calorie spray cooking oil

1 tbsp **dried sage**

1 tbsp **dried thyme**

1 tbsp **dried basil**

2 sticks **celery**, chopped

½ **fresh chilli**, deseeded and finely chopped

1 **chicken stock cube**, dissolved in 500ml water

1 **vegetable stock cube**, dissolved in 500ml water

salt and **pepper**, to taste

1. Preheat the oven to 200°C/180°C fan/gas mark 6. Line a baking tray with baking paper.

2. Lay the squash, peppers, onion halves and garlic on the tray and spray with oil to coat. Sprinkle with a pinch of salt and most of the sage, thyme and basil.

3. Roast in the oven for 40 minutes.

4. Spray some oil in a saucepan, add the chopped onions and sweat for 5 minutes over a low heat. Add the celery and chilli and sweat for a further 10 minutes until they are soft.

5. Once the roast vegetables are ready, add them (with their juices) to the onions and celery. Scoop out the flesh from the squash for a smooth soup, or chop if you'd like extra nutrition from the rind.

6. Add the stock and the rest of the sage, thyme and basil.

7. Bring to the boil, then reduce the heat to low and simmer for 20 minutes. Take off the heat and allow to cool.

8. Once the soup has cooled, blend until smooth and add salt and pepper to taste.

Jen's Protein Caesar Bowl

SERVES 2

432 **70g**

PER PORTION

This recipe is such a classic and so easy to make at home. It makes a great lunch for two or a dinner for one. Salads never have to be boring, and this one is packed with protein too!

2 skinless **chicken breasts**

4 **bacon medallions**

1 slice **wholemeal bread**

low-calorie spray cooking oil

1 **iceberg** or **Cos lettuce**, torn into large pieces

1 **scallion**, chopped

Caesar dressing (see page 265)

Parmesan, grated, to garnish

1. Preheat the grill.

2. Tenderise the chicken breasts using a meat mallet, or place them in a Ziplock bag and use a rolling pin. Cut the chicken into chunks and the bacon into strips.

3. Pop the chicken and bacon under the grill on a lined tray. Grill the chicken for 8 minutes on each side. Grill the bacon until crisp; this should only take around 4 minutes each side.

4. Meanwhile, cut the bread into small cubes, lightly coat with low-calorie spray cooking oil and toast in a dry pan on a medium heat until crisp.

5. Put the lettuce and chopped scallion in a serving bowl, add the chicken, bacon and dressing and toss everything together. Serve in two bowls, topped with the croutons and some grated Parmesan.

Spicy Mayo Tuna Bowl

498 **KCAL**   32g **PROTEIN**

This is a great lunch to throw together if you have some leftover rice, and it's lovely either warm or cold. Really handy for lunchboxes and packed with flavour and protein.

50g **rice** (**brown** or **white long grain**)

145g **tin tuna steak** (or 1 tuna steak, cooked)

¼ **cucumber**, chopped

1 medium **avocado**, sliced

1 medium **carrot**, grated

1 tbsp **sliced jalapeños**, from a jar

For the spicy mayonnaise

30g **light mayonnaise**

1 tbsp **sriracha**

juice of ½ **lemon**

1 tsp reduced-salt **soy sauce**

1 tsp **rice vinegar**

1. Cook the rice according to the instructions on the packet. When it's cooked, fluff it up with a fork.

2. Fill the bottom of your bowl with rice, then add the tuna and vegetables.

3. For the spicy mayo, mix all the ingredients in a bowl and serve it on the side.

Middle Eastern-Style Salad

SERVES 2

250 KCAL · **12g** PROTEIN

PER PORTION

This salad makes a perfect lunch on its own or it can be served as an accompaniment; I especially love it with barbecues in the summer. The flavours are so fresh and clean, and it lasts well if kept covered in the fridge.

60g **bulgur wheat**

400g tin **chickpeas**, drained and rinsed

2 **scallions**, finely chopped

100g **cherry tomatoes**, halved

1 **cooked beetroot**, cubed

½ **cucumber**, finely chopped

1 **garlic clove**, crushed

juice of 1 **lemon**

1 tsp chopped **fresh dill**

1 tsp chopped **fresh parsley**

½ tsp **ground cumin**

salt and **pepper**

1. Rinse the bulgur wheat and place it in a heatproof bowl. Pour on enough boiling water to cover it. Cover the bowl with a lid or plate and leave for 30 minutes, or until the water is fully absorbed. Allow to cool.

2. When the bulgur wheat is cool, transfer it to a serving bowl and mix in the chickpeas, scallions, tomatoes, beetroot and cucumber.

3. Add the garlic, lemon juice, dill, parsley, cumin, salt and pepper, and toss to combine.

Open Toasties

I love making toasties in the air fryer, and open ones are best because I can load more toppings on each slice! Beef pastrami, mustard, Cheddar and rocket is my favourite. And cheese and tuna are great for protein.

Pizza Bagels

This is so easy to make and a great one for the kids. Spread some passata on a halved bagel or a wrap, load it with whatever you fancy and throw it in the air fryer or oven for 5 minutes at 190°C (170°C fan/gas mark 5).

QUICK LUNCH IDEAS

Supreme Chicken Sandwich Filler

SERVES 1

150
KCAL

20g
PROTEIN

This always reminds me of family parties when I was younger. My mam always made sandwiches, and this would have been one of the fillings. You can turn it into a salad by adding more greens.

60g sliced **chicken**

40g **Cos lettuce**, shredded

4 **cherry tomatoes**, diced

2 **scallions**, sliced

3 tbsp **light mayonnaise**

In a bowl, mix the chicken, lettuce, cherry tomatoes and scallions with the mayonnaise.

TIP

Make a big bowl of this and keep it in the fridge to use for lunches during the week.

QUICK LUNCH IDEAS

Scrambled Egg with Salmon and Dill

473 KCAL **42g** PROTEIN

Such a classic but so easy to do. You can change this up by adding different ingredients to the eggs. Some of my favourite combinations are cheese, tomato and bacon; chicken, mushroom, feta and spinach; and sundried tomato, pesto and mozzarella.

2 **eggs**
2 tbsp **low-fat milk**
2 slices of **brown bread**
100g **smoked salmon**
sprig of **fresh dill**
1 **lemon** wedge
salt and **cracked black pepper**

1. To make really good scrambled eggs, whisk 2 eggs in a bowl with 2 tbsp low-fat milk and any seasoning you want to use.

2. Put a non-stick frying pan over a low–medium heat and pour in the eggs. After less than a minute, the eggs will start to set. Stir them energetically with a spatula and keep stirring until the eggs are almost cooked through. Season the eggs with salt and pepper to taste.

3. Take the eggs off the heat while you toast your bread.

4. Serve with the smoked salmon to the side, a squeeze of lemon juice and a scattering of fresh dill.

This is my favourite meal of the day. Growing up, I always ate dinner at the table with my family, and it's important to me to carry that on with Carter. I love having him help me in the kitchen, too (when he feels like it!). I know it's hard when you are tired after a day's work and you have to go into the kitchen, away from family again, and prepare a big, complicated dinner. When I was writing this book, I made simple, easy-to-prepare dinners a main focus because I know I'd rather spend more time enjoying my dinner with Carter than I would preparing it on my own. But simple doesn't mean boring. I try to incorporate lots of different flavours in my meals with spices, herbs and seasonings. You don't need an entire spice shop, but once you have the basics you can go so much further with your recipes.

Dinners

Everyone's Favourite Enchiladas

MAKES 6

415 KCAL   **30g** PROTEIN

PER ENCHILADA

I've been making this recipe for as long as I can remember. Living in London as a student, I always found it great for batch-cooking – it goes a long way and is great value for money. For me, it's real comfort food, and I always go the extra mile with the sides – guacamole, salsa, sour cream, refried beans or rice. My dad always says this is his favourite meal that I cook!

500g 5%-fat **beef mince**

1 **onion**, chopped

2 **garlic cloves**, minced

1 **red bell pepper**, sliced

1 tsp **chilli powder**

1 tsp **cayenne pepper**

1 tsp **ground cumin**

1 tsp **paprika**

1 **beef stock cube**, crumbled

400g tin **chopped tomatoes**

2 tbsp **tomato purée**

400g tin **kidney beans**, drained and rinsed

1 square **dark chocolate**

1. Preheat the oven to 190°C/170°C fan/gas mark 5.

2. Put the mince in a large pot over a medium heat. There is no need for oil as the mince will cook in its own fat. Use a spatula to break up the mince and fry it off until it begins to brown. I always drain off the excess fat. (Never pour it down the drain, as it will clog it, but keep an old jar for the purpose and pour the fat into it.)

3. Then add the onion, garlic and red pepper and cook on a low heat for 5 minutes until they begin to soften.

4. Add the chilli powder, cayenne, cumin and paprika, the crumbled stock cube, chopped tomatoes, tomato purée and kidney beans to the mince, and stir over a low–medium heat for a couple of minutes.

5. Add a square of rich dark chocolate and reduce the heat to low. Put the lid on and simmer for 15–20 minutes.

JEN'S FAVOURITE

For the enchilada sauce

1 **onion**, very finely chopped

low-calorie spray cooking oil

500ml **passata**

100ml **water**

2 tbsp **sweetener**

1–2 tsp **hot chilli powder**

1 tsp **cayenne pepper**

1 tsp **ground cumin**

1 tsp **paprika**

1 tsp **dried oregano**

1 tsp **garlic powder**

6 **wraps**

200g **reduced-fat Cheddar cheese**, grated

salad, **chives**, **sour cream** and **guacamole**, to serve

6. For the enchilada sauce, fry off the chopped onion in some low-calorie spray oil on a medium heat until soft and translucent. Add all the other ingredients, bring to the boil, then reduce the heat and simmer for 15 minutes.

7. Take each wrap, spoon some of the chilli over it (it's fine if it's cold) and roll it up. Lay the rolls out in a large baking dish and cover them with the enchilada sauce. Scatter the cheese over the top.

8. Cover with tinfoil and put in the oven for about 30 minutes. Serve with salad, chives, sour cream and guacamole.

Carbonara, but Cheating

SERVES 4

616 KCAL   **50.5g** PROTEIN

PER PORTION

I usually make this recipe with leftover ham, which I've cooked in the slow cooker, so then all I have to do is either dice it up or shred it. Always served with spaghetti, of course.

500g **cooked ham**

200g **dried spaghetti**

2 **onions**, finely chopped

2 **garlic cloves**, finely chopped

low-calorie spray cooking oil

1 **chicken stock cube**, dissolved in 100ml **water**

300g **frozen garden peas**

200g **light cream cheese**

cracked black pepper

fresh parsley, chopped, to garnish

Parmesan, to garnish

1. If you are cooking the ham from scratch on the same day, I would recommend putting it in a slow cooker for a few hours on a medium heat. If you are cooking it on the hob, put it in a large pot, cover with cold water and bring to a boil. Then simmer, with a lid on, for 40 minutes. Once the ham is cooked and cooled, shred it with two forks.

2. Cook the spaghetti while you get on with the sauce.

3. In a large pot, soften the onions and garlic in some low-calorie spray oil on a medium heat for 5 minutes. Add in the stock and frozen peas and simmer on a low–medium heat for 10 minutes.

4. Add the ham and remove from the heat. Stir in the cream cheese and add plenty of black pepper.

5. Drain the spaghetti, add the carbonara sauce and mix well.

6. Garnish with parsley and Parmesan.

Beef Stroganoff

SERVES 4

404 KCAL   **53g** PROTEIN

PER PORTION

This is one of my favourite dinners in the colder months. I usually serve it with rice, but it's lovely with a side of greens or mashed potatoes.

800g **lean stewing beef**, chopped

1 **beef stock cube**, dissolved in 500ml **water**

1 tbsp **dried thyme**

low-calorie spray cooking oil

3 **onions**, chopped

200g **mushrooms**, sliced

4 **garlic cloves**, finely chopped

3 tbsp **tomato purée**

1 tbsp **Worcestershire sauce**

1 tbsp **balsamic vinegar**

1 tsp **Dijon mustard**

1 tsp **paprika**

salt and **pepper**

100g **fat-free fromage frais** or **natural yoghurt** (see tip)

1. Place the beef in the slow cooker along with 250ml of the beef stock and the thyme, and cook on a medium heat for 4 hours. Alternatively, you can cook the stewing beef in a heavy-bottom pot with the stock and thyme for 1.5 to 2 hours on low until fork-tender.

2. Half an hour before the beef is finished, fry the onions, mushrooms and garlic in some spray oil in a deep pan over a medium–low heat until they are soft and lightly browned.

3. Add a few tablespoons of the reserved stock to the onions, garlic and mushrooms, and turn the heat up to high to reduce the liquid. Each time the mixture is almost dry, add in a little more stock until you have used it all.

4. Stir in the tomato purée, Worcestershire sauce, balsamic vinegar, mustard, 1 tsp paprika and salt and pepper.

5. Add the cooked beef and stock and remove from the heat.

6. Stir in the fromage frais or yoghurt and serve.

TIP

I usually leave my fromage frais out of the fridge for a few hours so that it's close to room temperature to avoid curdling when it goes into the hot beef mixture.

Jumbo Spicy Beef Sausage Rolls

MAKES 4

647 KCAL   **46g** PROTEIN

PER SAUSAGE ROLL

These are great for the family to enjoy. You can slice them up and serve them at parties too. They're great hot or cold, so they're perfect for lunchboxes. In this recipe, I've added some cheese and spice for extra flavour, but you can make them plain or add some chutney. I use lean mince to get my protein in; just be careful not to overcook them, as they can dry out.

500g 5%-fat **beef mince**

120g grated **Cheddar cheese**

handful **pickled jalapeños**, from a jar, chopped

1 sheet **ready-made light puff pastry**, cut into four squares

1 **egg**, beaten

rocket and **gherkins**, to serve

1. Preheat the oven to 190°C/170°C fan/gas mark 5.

2. In a bowl, mix together the mince, grated cheese and chopped jalapeños. Divide the mixture into four and form each into a long sausage shape.

3. Lay each sausage on one side of a pastry square and roll it up, carefully folding in the sides. Press a fork around the edges to seal them.

4. Brush the tops with a little beaten egg and cook for about 20–25 minutes until golden brown and crisp.

5. Serve with some rocket, gherkins and a dipping sauce. (See pages 258–270 for my favourite sauces.)

Cheese-Stuffed Spicy Meatballs

SERVES 4

400 **52g**

KCAL PROTEIN

PER PORTION

This is a little bit different from the usual and has a bit of a kick. I find pasta and meat dishes very filling, so a few of these meatballs go a long way.

800g 5%-**beef mince**

2 tbsp finely chopped
pickled jalapeños, from a jar

1 tsp **paprika**

1 tsp **dried oregano**

1 tsp **dried basil**

1 tsp **onion granules**

100g **light Cheddar cheese**,
cut into 20 cubes

For the sauce

1 **onion**, finely diced

2 **garlic cloves**, chopped

1 **red bell pepper**, diced

100g **mushrooms**, diced

1 tbsp **dried basil**

1 tbsp **dried oregano**

1 tbsp **dried parsley**

½ tsp **chilli flakes**

400g tin **chopped tomatoes**

2 tbsp **tomato purée**

1 **vegetable stock pot**

small handful **fresh basil**,
to garnish

1. Preheat the oven to 190°C/170°C fan/gas mark 5.

2. For the meatballs, mix the beef mince with the jalapeños, paprika, oregano, basil and onion granules.

3. Take a small ball of mince, put it in the palm of your hand and flatten it out. Then place a cube of cheese in the centre, wrap the mince around the cheese to cover it, and then mould it into a meatball. You should end up with 20 meatballs.

4. Put them on a baking tray and cook in the oven for about 15 minutes, shaking the tray halfway through so that they're browned all over.

5. While the meatballs are cooking, make the sauce. Spray a pan with cooking oil and soften the onion and garlic over a medium heat.

6. Add the pepper. After 5 minutes, add the mushrooms, basil, oregano, parsley, chilli flakes, tinned tomatoes, tomato purée and the stock pot. Simmer for 20 minutes.

7. Once the sauce is cooked, add the meatballs and scatter over some basil. Serve with pasta or on their own.

Lovely Layered Lasagne

SERVES 6

400 KCAL
43g PROTEIN

PER PORTION

This is definitely in my top favourite meals ever. My entire family clean their plates every time I make it, and it's so worth the effort. It's filling, too, and packed with lots of flavour.

1 large **onion**, chopped

2 **garlic cloves**, chopped

800g 5%-fat **beef mince**

1 **red bell pepper**, chopped

120g **mushrooms**, chopped

2 tsp **dried parsley**

1 tsp **dried oregano**

1 tsp **dried basil**

½ tsp **dried rosemary**

400g tin **chopped tomatoes**

1½ tbsp **tomato purée**

1 **reduced-salt beef stock cube**

1 **beef stock pot**

1 tbsp **Worcestershire sauce**

20g **packet white sauce mix**

280ml **low-fat milk**

6 **dry lasagne sheets**

200g **light mozzarella cheese**, grated

cracked black pepper

1. Preheat the oven to 190°C/170°C fan/gas mark 5.

2. Sauté the onions and garlic in a large pot over a medium heat until soft. Add in the mince and break it up with a spatula.

3. Once the meat is lightly browned, drain off the excess fat.

4. Add the red pepper, mushrooms, parsley, oregano, basil, rosemary, chopped tomatoes, tomato purée, stock cube, stock pot and Worcestershire sauce. Simmer on low for 15 minutes.

5. For the white sauce, whisk the powder into the milk in a pot, bring to the boil, whisking continuously, and then reduce to a simmer. Keep whisking until the sauce thickens – it will take about 5 minutes.

6. Put half the mince in a layer in a baking dish, cover with three lasagne sheets, then half the white sauce and top with about a quarter of the cheese.

7. Repeat these steps, finishing with the remaining cheese. Sprinkle with cracked black pepper and cover the dish with tinfoil.

8. Put in the oven for about 40 minutes. Take the foil off for the last 10 minutes to brown the cheese.

JEN'S FAVOURITE

Imperfectly Perfect Homemade Pizza

MAKES 1 PIZZA

542 KCAL   **32g** PROTEIN

Who doesn't love pizza? This is so easy and so tasty – it's Carter's favourite recipe in the whole book. We make this together all the time and it's a great way to get the whole family involved. It's a perfect weekend dinner. It goes without saying that you can add whatever toppings you like!

100g **self-raising flour**

100g **fat-free natural yoghurt**

low-calorie spray cooking oil

2 tbsp **tomato purée** mixed with 1 tsp **dried Italian seasoning** (see tip)

40g **light mozzarella cheese**, grated

2 **mushrooms**, sliced

1 slice of **ham**, torn into strips

1. Preheat the oven to 200°C/180°C fan/gas mark 6.

2. In a bowl, mix the flour and yoghurt with a spatula. (You can make the pizza smaller or larger, just make sure you use equal amounts of flour and yoghurt.) Keep mixing and mixing for about 5 minutes until it is dough-like and can be shaped with your hands. The mixture can be sticky, but the more you work it, the easier to handle it becomes.

3. I use my hands to pull it out into an imperfect pizza shape. You can most definitely use a rolling pin to get a larger, thinner base. (I would recommend using more flour, so the mixture doesn't stick to the rolling pin.)

4. Spray a little oil on some baking paper and lay the pizza base on it. Cook in the oven for 5 minutes on each side. Take it out, add the sauce and toppings and cook for a further 10 minutes.

TIP

You can make Italian seasoning by mixing together equal amounts of dried basil, oregano, thyme and rosemary.

JEN'S FAVOURITE

Red Wine Chorizo Pasta

SERVES 2

638 KCAL   **28g** PROTEIN

PER PORTION

This is so delicious I'd happily eat it every day. Cooking with chorizo is a great way to add some flavour to your pasta and veggies. This is a good one for batch cooking, and any leftovers can be used for lunches.

150g **dried fusilli**

100g **chorizo**, chopped

1 **onion**, chopped

2 **garlic cloves**, chopped

1 **red wine stock pot** or a splash of **red wine**

6 **mushrooms**, sliced

40g **olives**, pitted and halved

40g **sundried tomatoes**

200ml **tomato passata**

1 tsp **Worcestershire sauce**

handful **fresh basil**, to garnish

mozzarella, grated, to garnish (optional)

1. Cook the pasta while you prep the sauce.

2. Slowly cook the chorizo in a pan – no oil needed – on a low–medium heat. After 5 minutes, add the onion and continue to cook, stirring, for 3 minutes. Add the garlic, and keep stirring for a further 5 minutes, until the onion and garlic are soft.

3. Add the red wine stock pot or wine and a splash of water and stir well.

4. Add the mushrooms and continue to cook. When they've softened, add the olives and sundried tomatoes along with the passata and Worcestershire sauce.

5. Mix the drained pasta into the chorizo sauce.

6. Garnish with basil and grated mozzarella, if using.

TIP

The best way to cook dry pasta is to bring plenty of salted water to the boil – you need enough water to completely cover the pasta – add the pasta, bring it back to a quick boil, reduce to a simmer and give it a stir every few minutes.

Creamy Garlic and Mushroom Pasta

SERVES 4

350
KCAL

19g
PROTEIN

PER PORTION

Pasta in a white sauce is one of my favourites. I found a lot of these recipes require cream and butter and lots of high-calorie foods, which is fine, but I was really trying to stick to a plan. I made a few attempts at a simple creamy white mushroom sauce, and this recipe is the final result!

2 **onions**, chopped

low-calorie spray cooking oil

600g **button mushrooms**, quartered

2 **garlic cloves**, chopped

40g **plain flour**

300ml **low-fat milk**

1 **chicken stock cube**

1 **white wine stock pot** or a splash of **white wine**

250g **dried spaghetti**

fresh parsley, to garnish

cracked black pepper

1. Cook the chopped onions in a pan with some low-calorie spray cooking oil over a medium heat. When they begin to soften, add in the mushrooms and garlic and continue to cook on a medium heat for 5 minutes, stirring.

2. Sift the flour into the pan and keep mixing for a few minutes. It will look thick and messy, but go with it.

3. Pour the milk over the mixture and gently increase the heat, still stirring.

4. Crumble in the chicken stock cube and the white wine stock pot or white wine. Keep stirring. Once it starts to boil, reduce the heat and continue to cook, stirring, for a further 5 minutes until you have a smooth creamy sauce.

5. Cook and drain the spaghetti and mix with the sauce. Add some black pepper and serve, garnished with parsley.

Creamy Mushroom Peppered Chicken

SERVES 4

360 · **70g**

KCAL · PROTEIN

PER PORTION

This is another favourite; it's so easy to make and packed with protein. I usually serve it with green beans, crispy kale and rice or cauliflower rice (see page 251). Remember, a teaspoon of peppercorns can be quite hot!

1 **chicken stock cube**, dissolved in 1l **water**

4 large **skinless chicken breasts**, diced

low-calorie spray cooking oil

2 **onions**, chopped

400g **mushrooms**, chopped

1 **beef stock cube**, dissolved in 150ml **water**

1 tsp **black peppercorns**

200g **light cream cheese**

fresh parsley, to garnish

1 tsp **cracked black pepper**

1. Bring the chicken stock to the boil, then reduce to a simmer and add the diced chicken. The chicken will only take about 10 minutes to cook through. Do not add the raw chicken to boiling stock as it will make it dry.

2. Sweat the chopped onion and half the mushrooms on a pan over a low heat in a little oil for 10 minutes until they're soft. Put them in a blender, along with the beef stock and peppercorns. Blend until smooth.

3. Using the same pan, soften the rest of the mushrooms. When they're cooked, add in the sauce and the drained, poached chicken.

4. Remove from the heat and stir in the cream cheese.

5. Garnish with parsley and cracked black pepper.

Perfect Pesto and Gnocchi

325

KCAL

13g

PROTEIN

PER PORTION

Pasta, cheese and pesto make me happy. This pesto is perfect for serving over veggies when roasting, over a jacket potato, on toast with poached eggs or mixed through scrambled eggs. I love to mix mine with some light mayo for a lovely dip.

1 handful **fresh basil**

5 handfuls **spinach**

2 **garlic cloves**

juice of 1 **lemon**

2 tbsp **olive oil**

1 tbsp **pine nuts**

1 tbsp **sunflower seeds**

1 tbsp **nutritional yeast**

sea salt, to taste

500g bag **gnocchi**

low-calorie cooking spray oil

200g **mushrooms**, sliced

120g light **Cheddar cheese**, grated

1. Blend the basil, spinach, garlic, lemon juice, oil, nuts, seeds, yeast and salt in a food processor or blender. You may need to add a few drops of water to loosen it.

2. Bring a large pot of lightly salted water to the boil. Drop in the gnocchi and cook for 3–5 minutes or until the gnocchi rises to the top.

3. In a separate pot, cook the mushrooms for 5 minutes until soft.

4. Once the gnocchi are cooked, drain and add in the mushrooms and the pesto and stir well.

5. Serve up, add some Cheddar to each dish and stir well to melt the cheese.

TIP

This pesto can be kept in a sealed container in the fridge for about five days, or frozen in an ice cube tray.

Veggie Sausage Cheesy Pasta Bake

SERVES 4

444
KCAL

29g
PROTEIN

PER PORTION

Use whatever sausages you like: I like vegetarian ones because most of them have a lovely herby flavour, which goes well with this dish. Perfect for leftovers the next day or for batch cooking.

125g **cherry tomatoes**, halved

low-calorie spray cooking oil

sea salt and **black pepper**

1 tbsp **dried basil**

6 **sausages**

200g **dried fusilli** or **conchiglie**

1 **onion**, chopped

200g **mushrooms**, quartered

2 **garlic cloves**, chopped

2 tbsp **tomato purée**

dash of **Worcestershire sauce**

80g **mozzarella**, grated

100g **sundried tomatoes**

1. Preheat the grill.

2. Halve the tomatoes and lay them on a baking tray, cut side up. Spray with oil, season, sprinkle over the basil and grill for 30 minutes or until the tomatoes have collapsed.

3. When the tomatoes have been under the grill for about 15 minutes, move them to one side of the tray, add the sausages and cook them for the remaining 15 minutes.

4. Meanwhile, cook your pasta.

5. Spray a frying pan with a little oil and fry off the chopped onion on a low–medium heat until just softened, about 3 minutes. Then add the mushrooms and the garlic. Cut the sausages into chunks and add.

6. Once the mushrooms and garlic have softened, add the grilled tomatoes, tomato purée and Worcestershire sauce. Keep stirring until the mixture has a sauce-like texture.

7. Add the drained pasta to the sauce and stir.

8. Transfer to an oven dish. Sprinkle with the mozzarella and sundried tomatoes. Cover with tinfoil and bake for 20 minutes.

Pesto Chicken and Halloumi

SERVES 4

505
KCAL

75.5g
PROTEIN

PER PORTION

This dinner is real comfort food for me because three of my favourites are in it – chicken, pesto and halloumi. I made this a lot when I moved out on my own. When I started my journey, I didn't stop eating the meals I loved; I was just more mindful about portions.

1 **chicken stock pot**, dissolved in 1l **water**

4 **skinless chicken breasts**, diced

200g **white rice** (or **cauliflower rice** – see tip)

low-calorie spray cooking oil

2 **onions**, chopped

200g **button mushrooms**, quartered

200g **halloumi**

4 tbsp **pesto** (see recipe on page 193)

handful **cherry tomatoes**

fresh basil, to garnish

1. Bring the chicken stock to the boil, then reduce to a simmer and add the diced chicken. The chicken will only take about 10 minutes to cook through, and honestly it will be the juiciest, softest chicken. Do not add raw chicken to boiling water as it will make it dry.

2. Cook the white rice according to the instructions on the packet. Drain. (If you're using frozen cauliflower rice, pop it in the microwave.)

3. On a separate pan, soften the onion, the mushrooms and the halloumi in a little oil.

4. Throw in the cooked rice (or cauliflower rice) along with the pesto.

5. Add in some halved cherry tomatoes to heat through, then add the drained cooked chicken and give it a stir for a couple of minutes.

6. Serve with fresh basil leaves on top.

TIP

You can make your own cauliflower rice at home (see page 251). Store the 'rice' in an airtight container in the freezer. Then when you are ready to use it you can cook it from frozen.

JEN'S FAVOURITE

Chicken and Broccoli Bake

SERVES 4

375 **46.5g**

KCAL · PROTEIN

PER PORTION

Perfect for a Monday evening using leftover chicken from a Sunday roast, this dinner always reminds me of childhood. It's a great way to get two meals out of one and cut down on food waste, but it is just as easy to make with chicken breasts too. I usually have this on its own or with a side of veg.

3 **skinless chicken breasts**, diced

1 **chicken stock cube** dissolved in 1l **water**

300ml **low-fat milk**

1 tbsp **plain flour**

½ tsp **garlic powder**

120g **light Cheddar cheese**, grated

salt and **pepper**

1 head of **broccoli**, cut into small florets

low-calorie spray cooking oil

1 **onion**, chopped

1 **garlic clove**, chopped

1 slice **bread**, blitzed into breadcrumbs

1. Preheat the oven to 190°C/170°C fan/gas mark 5.

2. Bring the chicken stock to the boil, then reduce to a simmer and add the diced chicken. The chicken will only take about 10 minutes to cook through. Do not add the raw chicken to boiling water, as it will make it dry.

3. While the chicken's poaching, in a large pot, whisk the milk, flour and garlic powder together well, then place on a medium heat. Just as it begins to gently bubble, drop the heat and whisk for 3 to 5 minutes until it thickens.

4. Remove from the heat and add three-quarters of the grated cheese and salt and pepper to taste.

5. In a clean pot, boil the broccoli for no more than 5 minutes. Meanwhile, in a pan, soften the chopped onion and garlic in some spray oil and cook for 5 minutes.

6. Put the drained chicken, onion, garlic and broccoli in an oven dish. Pour the sauce on top and sprinkle over the breadcrumbs and the remaining cheese.

7. Cook in the oven for 25 minutes.

Southern Chicken Loaded Fries

SERVES 4

335 KCAL · **47g** PROTEIN

PER PORTION

These are one of the things I ate a lot of throughout my journey. If you haven't tried chips, chicken, cheese and gravy, here's exactly how you do it!

4 large **potatoes**, cut into chips

low-calorie spray cooking oil

4 **skinless chicken breasts**, sliced into strips

1 **onion**, sliced into rings

50g **light Cheddar cheese**, grated

100g **southern-style gravy powder**, whisked in a saucepan with 500ml **water**

fresh parsley, to garnish

For the crumb coating:

½ tsp **salt**

½ tsp **black pepper**

½ tsp **cayenne pepper**

½ tsp **paprika**

½ tsp **chives**

½ tsp **dried basil**

½ tsp **onion granules**

½ tsp **garlic powder**

2 slices **wholemeal bread**, blitzed into breadcrumbs

1. Preheat the oven to 200°C/180°C fan/gas mark 6.

2. Put the chips in a microwave-safe bowl and heat them in the microwave on high (800W) for about 5 minutes, then transfer them to a baking sheet, spray with oil and cook for about 30 minutes in the oven, shaking regularly.

3. Meanwhile, mix all the crumb coating ingredients together. Put about three-quarters of the mix in a plastic box with lid.

4. Add the chicken to the box, put on the lid and shake until fully coated. Lay the chicken slices on a baking tray and spray with some oil. Cook for about 10 minutes and then turn the chicken over.

5. While the chicken is cooking, put the onion slices into the lunchbox with the rest of the breadcrumbs and give it a good shake.

6. When you turn the chicken, lay the rings on the tray, spray them with oil and cook for about another 10 minutes.

7. Plate up the chips, chicken and crispy onions, add the cheese on top and drizzle the gravy all over.

JEN'S FAVOURITE

Meatza Pizza

484 KCAL · **101g** PROTEIN

This is my riff on pizza – with lots of extra protein! Handy when I need a quick one-tray dish for myself and Carter that's still packed with goodness. I love chicken and never find it boring because there are so many ways to funk it up. These are surprisingly filling, and I usually have them with a salad.

1 **skinless chicken breast**

2 tbsp **tomato purée**

½ tsp **dried basil**

½ tsp **dried oregano**

½ tsp **salt**

½ tsp **black pepper**

3 **mushrooms**, sliced

40g **ham**

40g **light Cheddar cheese**, grated

1. Preheat the oven to 190°C/170°C fan/gas mark 5.

2. Tenderise each side of the breast to make it a more even thickness. I do this with a meat mallet. If you don't have a mallet, just throw your chicken into a Ziploc bag, squeeze out the air and hammer it with a rolling pin.

3. To make the sauce, mix the tomato puree, basil, oregano, salt and pepper with a teaspoon of water. Spread some of the tomato sauce on the chicken breast.

4. Add the mushrooms and ham (or whatever toppings you like) and all the cheese. Place on a baking tray lined with baking paper. Cook in the oven for 15–20 minutes or until cooked through.

Smoky BBQ Pulled Chicken

SERVES 4

218
KCAL

45g
PROTEIN

PER PORTION

You should make this immediately! It can be made with chicken or pork – but whichever you decide, the sauce is delicious. It's an ideal slow cooker meal because everything is thrown together and left to cook for the day, and in the evening, you'll have the softest, tastiest meat that can be used in lots of different ways. It's a perfect family meal, and it freezes well too.

4 skinless chicken breasts

1 chicken stock cube dissolved in 1l **water** (if not using a slow cooker)

low-calorie spray cooking oil (if not using a slow cooker)

1 large **onion**, chopped

2 **garlic cloves**, chopped

500ml **passata**

1 rich and smoky stock pot (available from Tesco) or a **beef Oxo cube**

2 tbsp **apple cider vinegar** (or **balsamic vinegar**)

1 tbsp **Worcestershire sauce**

1 tsp **Dijon mustard**

1 tsp **paprika**

1 to 2 tsp **chipotle powder** or **cayenne pepper**

1. If you have a slow cooker, just throw everything into it and cook on medium for about 5 hours. If you don't have a slow cooker, bring the chicken stock to the boil, then reduce to a simmer and add the chicken breasts. The chicken will only take about 10 to 15 minutes to cook through. Do not add the raw chicken to boiling stock as it will make it dry.

2. Spray a large pan with some low-calorie spray cooking oil and sweat the onion and garlic over a low heat for 10 minutes. Then add the passata, stock pot or stock cube, vinegar, Worcestershire sauce, mustard, paprika and chipotle powder or cayenne pepper and simmer gently for 20 minutes.

3. Shred the chicken with two forks, add to the sauce and stir through.

4. Serve in a burrito or on a baked potato topped with grated light cheese and chives.

Hot Barbecue Boneless Chicken Bites

SERVES 4

266 **63.5g**

KCAL   PROTEIN

PER PORTION

These are like delicious, sticky popcorn chicken bites. You can have them on their own or with some chips, in a wrap or as part of a salad. We love these because you can change the flavour of the coating so easily by mixing different sauces together, and even though they are so simple to make, they taste like something from a restaurant.

6 **skinless chicken breasts**, cut into bite-sized chunks

60g **panko breadcrumbs**

pinch of **salt**

1 tbsp **lemon and pepper seasoning** (I get mine in SuperValu)

1 tsp **garlic powder**

1 tsp **onion powder**

low-calorie spray oil

2 tbsp **hot wings sauce** (Cali Cali Hot Wings Sauce is my go-to)

1 tbsp **barbecue sauce** (see the recipe on page 258)

garlic sauce, to serve (see the recipe on page 269)

1. Preheat the oven to 200°C/180°C fan/gas mark 6. If using an air fryer, preheat it (for about 3 minutes) to 200°C.

2. Throw the chicken into a plastic box with a lid along with the breadcrumbs, salt, lemon and pepper seasoning, garlic powder and onion powder. Give the lunchbox a good shake, making sure that all the chicken is coated.

3. Spray the chicken pieces with oil and cook in the oven or air fryer for about 15 minutes, shaking or turning them a few times.

4. Mix the hot wings sauce and barbecue sauce in a bowl, throw in the cooked crispy chicken bites and coat them all in the sauce.

5. Serve with the garlic sauce on the side.

Crispy Golden Chicken Goujons

SERVES 4

285

KCAL

65g

PROTEIN

PER PORTION

I found that once I started making my own breaded chicken goujons, I very rarely bought ready-made ones any more. They're so easy to make, they're healthier, and they freeze really well. They're lovely served with corn on the cob (see page 253) and coleslaw (page 262). Carter and I also love them in a wrap for lunch.

3 slices of **bread**

1 tsp **dried oregano**

1 tsp **paprika**

1 tsp **cayenne pepper**

½ tsp **garlic powder**

½ tsp **onion granules**

salt and **black pepper**

6 skinless **chicken breasts**, sliced into strips

low-calorie spray cooking oil

1. Preheat the oven to 190°C/170°C fan/gas mark 5.

2. Blitz the bread in a food processor to make breadcrumbs. Throw in all the other ingredients apart from the chicken and oil, and blend again. You can add as much or as little of each spice and herb as you like – experiment until you find the combination you like best!

3. Put half the breadcrumbs in a large plastic box with a lid, add half the chicken, put the lid on and shake until all the chicken is covered with breadcrumbs. Repeat with the rest of the breadcrumbs and the rest of the chicken.

4. Cover a baking tray with some tinfoil and spray with a little oil. Lay the chicken strips on the tray and spray with a little more oil.

5. Cook in the oven for 20 minutes, turning once. Increase the temperature to 200°C (180°C fan/gas mark 6) for the final 5 minutes to make the chicken strips crisper.

Sweet Chilli Hoisin Boneless Chicken Bites

SERVES 4

280 KCAL 63g PROTEIN

PER PORTION

You can probably tell I love a boneless chicken bite, and some of the coatings I put on the crispy bites are too good not to share!

6 **skinless chicken breasts**, cut into bite-sized chunks

60g **panko breadcrumbs** (or 2 slices of **bread**, blitzed into breadcrumbs)

salt, to taste

garlic sauce, to serve (see page 269)

For the sweet chilli hoisin sauce

1 tbsp **hoisin sauce**

1 tbsp **honey**

1 tbsp **soy sauce**

½ tsp **chilli flakes**

½ tsp **garlic granules**

½ tsp **ground ginger**

1. Preheat the oven to 200°C/180°C fan/gas mark 6. If using an air fryer, preheat it (for about 3 minutes) to 200°C.

2. Throw the chicken chunks into a container with a lid, along with the breadcrumbs and salt. Give the container a good shake, making sure that all the chicken is coated in breadcrumbs.

3. Spray the chicken with oil and cook on a baking tray in the oven or in the air fryer for about 15 minutes, giving them a few shakes or turns.

4. For the sweet chilli hoisin sauce, mix all the ingredients thoroughly and drizzle all over the cooked chicken bites.

Honey Chilli Crispy Chicken

SERVES 4

268 KCAL · **63g** PROTEIN

PER PORTION

Sometimes when I fancy takeaway food, this kind of recipe hits the spot. It tastes great, everyone loves it, and it's packed with protein. I've kept the ingredients as simple as possible because I want them to be accessible – most people will already have most of the ingredients in their kitchen. I love to serve this with chips or on a bed of rice with a side of greens.

40g **panko breadcrumbs**

1 tsp **onion granules**

1 tsp **paprika**

1 tsp **garlic powder**

6 **skinless chicken breasts**, sliced into strips

low-calorie spray cooking oil

1 **scallion**, finely sliced, to garnish

For the sauce

330ml **zero-sugar fizzy orange drink**

2 **garlic cloves**, finely chopped

1 tbsp **honey**

1 tbsp **Worcestershire sauce**

1 tbsp **soy sauce**

1 tsp **chilli flakes**

1. Mix the breadcrumbs, onion granules, paprika and garlic powder in a plastic box with a lid.

2. Put the chicken strips into the lunchbox and shake until evenly covered. Spray with some oil and cook in the air fryer at 200°C for 20 minutes, turning once. Alternatively, place under the grill for 20 minutes, turning once. Make sure the chicken is cooked through and golden and crisp on the outside.

3. In a pan, bring the fizzy orange drink to the boil and add the rest of the ingredients. Cook on a high heat for 10–15 minutes, stirring, until it has reduced to a thick sauce. Then add in your cooked crispy chicken and serve, garnished with sliced scallion.

TIP

If you don't want to use the fizzy orange, you can just add an extra 2 tablespoons of honey.

JEN'S FAVOURITE

Sweet and Sour in Half an Hour

SERVES 4

312 KCAL · **65g** PROTEIN

PER PORTION

This is absolutely delicious, and I've made it so many times I think I've perfected the sauce. It's really easy, too, I promise, and it can be made in less than twenty minutes. Served with white rice or chips, it tastes just like a takeaway.

6 skinless chicken breasts, diced

40g panko breadcrumbs

1 tsp **paprika**

low-calorie spray cooking oil

6 tbsp **apple cider vinegar**

3 tbsp **tomato ketchup**

2 tbsp **sweetener** (I like stevia leaf)

1 tbsp **tomato purée**

1 tbsp **Worcestershire sauce**

1 tsp **cornflour**

1 **onion**, cut into chunks

1 **red bell pepper**, cut into chunks

1 **scallion**, finely sliced, to garnish

1. Preheat the oven to 190°C/170°C fan/gas mark 5.

2. Throw the diced chicken, breadcrumbs and paprika into a plastic box with a lid. Pop the lid on and shake until all the chicken pieces are covered. Make sure each piece of chicken is evenly covered. It's easiest to do this in two batches.

3. Spray a baking tray with low-calorie spray oil and spread out the chicken pieces on it. Cook for 15 minutes, turning once, until cooked through and golden and crisp on the outside.

4. In a bowl, mix the apple cider vinegar, ketchup, sweetener, tomato purée, Worcestershire sauce and cornflour. Mix well until the sauce has a smooth consistency.

5. On a large frying pan, soften the onion and red pepper over a medium heat for 5 minutes. Once they're soft, throw in the crispy chicken pieces and pour in the sauce. Stir it all around until everything is covered in sauce. Serve straight away, garnished with the sliced scallion.

Chicken Katsu Curry

SERVES 4

525
KCAL

66.5g
PROTEIN

PER PORTION (WITH 150G COOKED WHITE RICE)

Chicken katsu curry is one of my favourite things to order when I eat out, so I wanted to recreate a version I would love just as much that I could make at home. There are so many variations and recipes online, but I played around with the ingredients for a long time, and this is the closest I've got to it tasting like the ones I order. Soup-based sauces are so handy because you get so much veg into them, there aren't a lot of calories in them, and you can make them as thick or as watery as you like (I like them thick!).

For the katsu sauce

low-calorie spray cooking oil

1 large **onion**, chopped

4 **garlic cloves**, chopped

2cm **fresh ginger**, peeled and finely chopped

2 **carrots**, chopped

1 **courgette**, chopped

2 tsp **ground cumin**

2 tsp **ground coriander**

1 tsp **chilli powder**

1 tsp **ground turmeric**

1 tbsp **sweetener** (e.g. stevia leaf)

1 **chicken stock cube**, dissolved in 800ml **water**

1 tbsp **soy sauce**

100ml **light coconut milk**

1. Start with the sauce. In a large pot sprayed with some low-calorie cooking oil, cook the onion, garlic and ginger on a medium heat until they are soft.

2. Add the chopped carrots and courgette and cook for another 5 minutes, then add the cumin, coriander, chilli powder, turmeric and sweetener and stir to combine.

3. Pour in the chicken stock and soy sauce, bring to the boil and then simmer for 30–40 minutes.

4. Allow to cool, then blend with a hand blender. Stir in the coconut milk.

5. Preheat the oven to 190°C/170°C fan/gas mark 5.

CONTINUED OVERLEAF ...

Chicken Katsu Curry

4 skinless **chicken breasts**

1 tsp **garlic granules**

1 tsp **smoked paprika**

1 tsp **cayenne pepper**

½ tsp **salt**

½ tsp **black pepper**

2 slices of **bread**, blitzed into breadcrumbs

1 **egg**, beaten

low-calorie spray cooking oil

200g **white rice**

Japanese pickled vegetables, cucumber and **lettuce** to serve

6. Tenderise the chicken by putting the breasts, one at a time, in a plastic bag and flattening with a rolling pin or mallet.

7. Mix the garlic granules, smoked paprika, cayenne, salt and pepper into the breadcrumbs and spread them out on a plate to make it easier to coat the chicken.

8. Line a baking tray with baking paper and spray with oil. Dip each chicken breast into the egg wash and then coat in the breadcrumbs. Put the chicken breasts on the tray and spray some more oil on the chicken.

9. Cook the chicken in the oven for about 20–25 minutes, turning once. Meanwhile, cook the rice according to the instructions on the packet.

10. Slice the breaded chicken and serve with the rice, pouring the sauce over the chicken, and with the Japanese pickles, cucumber and lettuce.

The Nation's Favourite Spice Bag

SERVES 4

390 · **70g**

KCAL PROTEIN

PER PORTION

Since the start of my journey, the spice bag has always been my most popular recipe. I play around with the recipe all the time, and I've developed this one, which tastes really good for very few calories. But to get some extra calories in, you can add chips or replace the cauliflower rice with regular rice.

For the spice mix

2 tsp **sea salt**

2 tsp **paprika**

2 tsp **cayenne pepper**

2 tsp **garlic powder**

2 tsp **onion granules**

2 tsp **dried oregano**

2 tsp **chilli powder**

1 tsp **ground ginger**

1 tsp **cracked black pepper**

6 **skinless chicken breasts**, sliced

40g **panko breadcrumbs** (regular breadcrumbs or 2 tbsp **cornflour** work well too)

low-calorie spray cooking oil

1. Preheat the oven to 200°C/180°C fan/gas mark 6. If using an air fryer, preheat it (for about 3 minutes) to 200°C.

2. Mix all the spice mix ingredients together. Throw the chicken slices into a plastic box with a lid together with the breadcrumbs and half the spice mix. Put the lid on the lunchbox and shake it. Make sure the chicken is evenly coated. You might find it easier to do this in two batches.

3. Spray the chicken with oil, spread it out on a baking tray and cook in the oven or air fryer for 15–20 minutes. You want it crisp but not overcooked, so that the chicken is still juicy on the inside. If you're using the oven, turn the chicken pieces once, halfway through. If you're using an air fryer, give the chicken a shake every 5 minutes.

CONTINUED OVERLEAF ...

JEN'S FAVOURITE

The Nation's Favourite Spice Bag

CONTINUED …

2 **onions**, sliced

3 **garlic cloves**, finely chopped

3 **scallions**, finely sliced

½ a **green bell pepper**, sliced

½ a **yellow bell pepper**, sliced

½ a **red bell pepper**, sliced

1 **fresh chilli**, deseeded and finely chopped

1 tbsp **soy sauce**

Chinese-style curry sauce (McDonnells do a Slimmer Curry Sauce, which is delicious), to serve (optional)

For the egg-fried cauliflower rice

2 portions of **cauliflower rice** (see page 251) – 1 portion is 200g (or see tip)

100g **frozen peas**

1 tbsp **soy sauce**

2 **eggs**

4. On a large pan, soften the onion in some spray oil and the remaining spice mix. When the onion has softened, add the garlic, scallions, peppers, chilli and soy sauce.

5. For the egg-fried cauliflower rice, throw the 'rice' into a pan with the frozen peas and a splash of soy sauce. Crack both eggs into the pan and keep mixing well until the eggs are cooked through.

6. When dishing up, I like to plate the rice first, and then the chicken topped with the onions and veg, and the curry sauce drizzled over. A side of chips (see page 250) goes perfectly too!

TIP

Green Isle do the handiest little microwaveable 200g portion-sized bags of cauliflower rice.

Chicken Curry

520 KCAL   **67.5g** PROTEIN

PER PORTION (WITH 150G COOKED WHITE RICE)

This curry, using a soup base, was one of the meals I made most frequently at the beginning of my journey. It is so easy, delicious and really low in calories and high in protein. The sauce can easily be made thicker by using less water or adding a little cornflour.

low-calorie spray cooking oil

3 large **onions**, 1 finely chopped, 2 roughly chopped

2 **carrots**, finely chopped

2 **garlic cloves**, finely chopped

3–4 tbsp **mild curry powder**

1 tbsp **garam masala**

1 tsp **cayenne pepper**

1 tsp **ground coriander**

1 tsp **ground turmeric**

1 tsp **chilli flakes**

2 **chicken stock pots**

4 **skinless chicken breasts**, diced

200g **mushrooms**, chopped

200g **white rice**

1. In a large pot, sweat the finely chopped onion, carrots and garlic on a low heat in a little spray oil for about 20 minutes until really soft.

2. Add the curry powder and spices and mix together. Continue to cook on a low heat for a few minutes to intensify the flavours.

3. Dissolve 1 chicken stock pot in 600ml boiling water, add to the pan and simmer for 20 minutes. Remove from the heat, allow to cool and blend with a hand blender until smooth.

4. Cook the rice in a separate pot.

5. Meanwhile, in a large pan or pot, dissolve a chicken stock pot in enough boiling water to cover the chicken, reduce the heat to a simmer and drop in the chicken. Simmer for about 10 to 15 minutes until cooked through.

6. In a separate pan, soften the remaining onions and the mushrooms over a low–medium heat for 10 minutes.

7. Add the poached chicken and curry sauce to the cooked vegetables and mix together.

Curry in a Hurry

SERVES 4

427
KCAL

64g
PROTEIN

PER PORTION

Chinese-style chicken and prawn curry in a hurry is one of my go-to recipes. I like a thick curry sauce, and this is just that. You can replace the baked beans with butter beans or cannellini beans, if you like.

2 large **onions**, chopped

low-calorie spray cooking oil

2 **garlic cloves**, finely chopped

10 medium-sized **mushrooms**, chopped

200g **frozen peas**

3 tbsp **curry powder**

1 **chicken stock cube**, dissolved in 1l **water**

4 **skinless chicken breasts**, diced

300g raw, peeled **prawns**

For the curry sauce
420g tin **baked beans**

400g tin **plum tomatoes**

420g tin **mushy peas**

2 tsp **garam masala**

1 tsp **chilli powder**

1 tsp **ground cumin**

1 tsp **ground turmeric**

1. Soften the chopped onions with a little oil in a medium-sized pot over a medium heat until soft. Add the garlic and mushrooms and continue to cook for 5 minutes. Then add the frozen peas and curry powder and cook on a low heat for a further 5 minutes.

2. To make the curry sauce, throw the beans, plum tomatoes and mushy peas into a separate large pot along with the garam masala, chilli powder, cumin and turmeric, and blend with a hand blender until smooth. Turn on the heat to a low-medium temperature to warm through.

3. Bring the stock to the boil in a separate pan, reduce the heat to low–medium and add the chicken. It shouldn't take more than 10 minutes to cook through. Don't add the chicken to boiling stock – this will dry it out. Reserve a cup of the chicken stock before draining.

4. Mix all the veg into the curry sauce and then spoon in the cooked chicken, add the prawns and heat through. If the sauce is thick for your liking, add in 100ml or so of the reserved stock.

5. Serve with rice.

Loaded Taco Fries

SERVES 6

405 KCAL

33g PROTEIN

PER PORTION

This recipe is perfect for using up leftover chilli or Bolognese sauce – you can just add the spices to switch it up. It's also great for batch cooking as it freezes really well. My favourite way to have the chilli is with homemade chips, but it's also great over a jacket potato or in a burrito. This is one of those dishes you can throw on a large dish and place in the middle of the table and let everyone help themselves.

For the chilli con carne
650g 5%-fat **beef mince**
2 **onions**, chopped
2 **garlic cloves**, chopped
2 **large bell peppers**, chopped
200g **mushrooms**, chopped
1 tsp **chilli powder**
1 tsp **cayenne pepper**
1 tsp **ground cumin**
1 tsp **paprika**
1 **Knorr chilli and tomato stock pot**
1 **beef stock cube**
400g tin **chopped tomatoes**
2 tbsp **tomato purée**
400g **taco beans** or **kidney beans**
1 large square of **dark chocolate**

1. Preheat the oven to 190°C/170°C fan/gas mark 5. If using an air fryer, preheat it (for about 3 minutes) to 190°C.

2. Fry off the mince in a pot (no oil needed) until it begins to brown, then drain off the excess fat.

3. Add the onion, garlic, pepper and mushrooms and cook on a low heat for 5 minutes.

4. Add the chilli powder, cayenne pepper, cumin and paprika and stock pot, crumble in the stock cube and mix well. Then add the chopped tomatoes, tomato purée and beans. Mix well and then – trust me – add a big square of rich dark chocolate.

5. Partially cover with a lid and simmer on a low heat for 20–30 minutes.

6 large **potatoes**, peeled and
cut into chips

low-calorie spray cooking oil

sea salt

taco sauce (see page 265)

grated cheese, to serve

6. Meanwhile, put the potatoes in a large
microwave-safe bowl and microwave on high for
5 minutes, shaking halfway through. Remove
them from the microwave and spray them evenly
with low-calorie cooking oil and sprinkle with
some sea salt if you like.

7. Cook them in the air fryer or oven for 30
minutes; give them a shake every 5 minutes to
make sure they cook evenly. They should be
golden and crisp.

8. Serve the chilli with the chips, taco sauce and
grated cheese.

Smasho Nacho

SERVES 4

551 KCAL

77.5g PROTEIN

PER PORTION

My take on nachos in this dish are the 'smashed' crispy baby potatoes. With chicken goujons, roasted peppers, melted cheese, scallions and a drizzle of taco sauce, this is pure comfort food.

800g **baby potatoes**

low-calorie spray cooking oil

2 tbsp **garlic and herb seasoning** (Cali Cali do a lovely one)

4 **chicken breasts**, cut into strips

40g **panko breadcrumbs**

1 tsp **smoked paprika**

1 tsp **garlic powder**

2 **peppers**, sliced

120g ready-made grated **light Cheddar cheese** and **mozzarella**

taco sauce (see page 265), to serve

1. Preheat the oven to 190°C/170°C fan/gas mark 5.

2. If using a bag of microwaveable potatoes, cook according to the instructions on the packet. Otherwise, parboil them for 3–5 minutes. Lay the microwaved or parboiled potatoes on a baking tray, squash them down with a fork or potato masher, spray with oil and sprinkle over the garlic and herb seasoning. Put them in the oven for 20–30 minutes, depending on how crisp you like them.

3. Place the sliced chicken in a plastic box with a lid with the panko breadcrumbs, smoked paprika and garlic powder. Put the lid on and shake the box until all the chicken pieces are covered.

4. Spray the chicken with oil, put on a baking tray with the sliced peppers and cook in the oven for 15–20 minutes.

5. Load the chicken and peppers on top of the baby potatoes and add the cheese on top while hot so that it melts. Serve with the taco sauce.

Hot and Spicy Crispy Chicken Burger

MAKES 1 BURGER

453 KCAL   **64g** PROTEIN

Honestly, this is one of the nicest burgers I've made. Chicken burgers are one of my favourite meals; they're a great way to feed the family and they're always satisfying and packed with protein.

½ slice **bread**, blitzed into breadcrumbs

1 tsp **lemon and pepper seasoning**

1 tsp **southern fried chicken seasoning** (Schwartz does a lovely one)

1 **skinless chicken breast**

low-calorie spray cooking oil

2 tbsp **hot wings sauce** (e.g. Cali Cali)

1 tsp **American mustard**

1 **brioche burger bun**

1 tbsp **Hellmann's Lighter than Light Mayonnaise**

iceberg lettuce, shredded

1. Preheat the oven to 200°C/180°C fan/gas mark 6.

2. Mix the breadcrumbs with the lemon and pepper seasoning and southern fried seasoning.

3. Tenderise the chicken breast by placing it in a Ziploc bag and flattening with a rolling pin or mallet.

4. Spread the breadcrumbs out on a plate and coat the chicken breast on both sides.

5. Spray with some oil, put on a baking tray and cook in the oven for 15–20 minutes, turning once.

6. Mix the hot wings sauce with the mustard and coat the cooked chicken in it.

7. Layer the burger on a brioche bun with mayo and shredded lettuce.

Jen's Protein Turkey Burgers

MAKES 4 BURGERS

120 KCAL

25.5g PROTEIN

PER BURGER

Turkey burgers are one of my go-to meals each week. They are so handy, and I love the fact that they are lean and high in protein. It took me a while to get used to the turkey mince – I found it could be dry and bland. But once you add some flavours and extra ingredients, it tastes really good. These burgers are juicy and delicious.

400g **lean turkey mince**

1 **egg**, beaten

½ **red bell pepper**, finely chopped

½ **onion**, finely chopped

2 tsp **dried chives**

1 tbsp **all-purpose seasoning** (see tip)

1 tsp **dried parsley**

1 tsp **paprika**

1. Preheat the oven to 190°C/170°C fan/gas mark 5.

2. Mix all the ingredients together in a bowl. Mould into four burger shapes and place on a lined baking tray.

3. Cook in the oven for 10–12 minutes on each side.

4. You can serve these in buns, like regular burgers, or with salad and guacamole or cheese.

TIP

If you find it hard to get your hands on all-purpose seasoning, it's quite easy to make yourself at home. In a small dish, mix together 1 tsp each of paprika, ground cumin, ground coriander, garlic powder, dried oregano and ½ tsp of black pepper.

Meat-Free Bites

MAKES 8 BITES

48
KCAL

3.3g
PROTEIN

PER BITE

I can't believe how easy these are to make, and I think if you make them you'll love them. I have made these with Carter and he loved getting involved. Alternatively, you could shape them into small balls and use them to fill pittas, together with some leaves, cucumber, tomatoes and tzatziki (see page 270).

400g tin **lentils**, drained and rinsed

1 **egg**

1 tsp **garlic granules**

1 tsp **paprika**

1 tsp **cayenne pepper**

1 slice of **bread**, blitzed into breadcrumbs

½ **scallion**, finely chopped

garlic sauce (see page 269), to serve

1. Preheat the grill. If using an air fryer, preheat it (for about 3 minutes) to 190°C.

2. In a bowl, mash the lentils with a potato masher until they are mushy but still have some texture.

3. Whisk the egg with the garlic granules, paprika and cayenne.

4. Pour the egg mixture into the mashed lentils along with the breadcrumbs and scallion.

5. Make 8 balls from the mix and press them down into burger shapes. Cook them in the air fryer or under the grill for 8–10 minutes each side.

TIP

You could make these vegan by replacing the egg with a couple of tablespoons of the water from the lentils and mashing the lentils a little more thoroughly.

Chickpea Burgers

MAKES 6 BURGERS

87 KCAL **4.3g** PROTEIN

PER BURGER

I like to have some meat-free meals during the week, and these are one of my favourite options. They're absolutely delicious hot or cold, and they can be used for lunches, in salads, or in buns or pittas with salad leaves, cucumber, tomatoes and garlic sauce. The mixture would be great shaped into bite-sized balls for a dinner party or for kids' lunchboxes.

400g tin **chickpeas**, drained and rinsed

juice of ½ **lime**

1 **red onion**, finely chopped

1 **garlic clove**, minced

1 tsp **dried oregano**

1 tsp **ground cumin**

1 tsp **cayenne pepper**

1 tsp **smoked paprika**

2 tbsp **plain flour**

1 **red bell pepper**, finely chopped

½ small tin **sweetcorn** (100g)

low-calorie spray cooking oil

Pittas, **salad** and **tzatziki** (see page 270), to serve

1. Use a potato masher to mash the chickpeas with the lime juice and salt and pepper. Add the finely chopped onion, garlic, oregano, cumin, cayenne pepper and paprika.

2. Sieve in the flour and mix well, then add the red pepper and sweetcorn.

3. Take golf-ball size pieces of the mixture and mould them into burger shapes. You should get 6 good-sized burgers.

4. Leave to chill for an hour or more in the fridge if you can.

5. Fry off in some spray oil on a medium heat for about 4 or 5 minutes on each side. And then finish in the air fryer or oven for about 10 minutes (turning once) at 190°, if you'd prefer a sturdier texture.

TIP

If you want to avoid using flour, you can use a beaten egg to bind the mixture.

Fakeaway Fish and Chips

SERVES 4

448 KCAL   **36g** PROTEIN

PER PORTION

This is one of those dinners that you would think requires a lot of effort, but it really doesn't. I usually serve it with my tartare sauce (page 265) – the perfect combo.

4 **carrots**, cut into chips

6 **potatoes**, cut into chips

salt and **pepper**

low-calorie spray cooking oil

3 slices of **bread**

1 tsp **dried dill**

1 tsp **garlic powder**

1 tsp **dried chives**

1 **egg**, beaten

4 **skinless cod fillets**, cut into chunks

low-calorie spray cooking oil

lemon wedges and some chopped **dill**, to garnish

1. Preheat the oven to 190°C/170°C fan/gas mark 5.

2. Put the carrots and potatoes in a microwave-safe bowl and microwave for 5 minutes. Season with salt and pepper, spray with oil and give them a good shake. Pop on a baking tray and cook in the oven for 45 minutes, shaking them from time to time.

3. Blitz the bread in a blender along with the dill, garlic powder and chives and pour into a bowl.

4. Dip each piece of fish in the beaten egg and then the breadcrumbs.

5. Lay the fish on a tray lined with baking paper and spray with oil.

6. Place in the oven for 15 to 20 minutes, turning once.

7. Serve your fish and chips with some lemon wedges, and garnish with chopped dill.

Seafood Tagliatelle

SERVES 4

481
KCAL

43g
PROTEIN

PER PORTION

Seafood and pasta go together so well. You can use whatever seafood you like or add extra prawns (I usually do). Seafood is great not only because it's nutritious but also because a lot of fresh seafood is low in calories and high in protein!

low-calorie spray cooking oil

200g **mushrooms**, chopped

2 **garlic cloves**, chopped

150g **frozen peas**

1 **fish stock cube**, dissolved in 100ml **water**

1 tsp **dried parsley**

juice of 1 **lemon**

500g **fresh seafood mix**

600g **tagliatelle**

1 tbsp **fat-free fromage frais**

15g **Parmesan**, grated

cracked black pepper and a few sprigs of **fresh dill**, to garnish

1. Soften the mushrooms and garlic in a pan with some spray oil over a low–medium heat for 5 minutes.

2. Add the frozen peas, fish stock, parsley and lemon juice. Mix together and then add the seafood mix and cook for about 7–8 minutes.

3. Meanwhile, cook the tagliatelle according to packet instructions.

4. In a bowl, mix the fromage frais and Parmesan with some black pepper.

5. Take the seafood off the heat, add the fromage frais mixture and stir well.

6. Drain the tagliatelle and mix with the seafood sauce. Serve with lots of cracked black pepper and some fresh dill.

TIP

Instead of fromage frais and grated Parmesan you could use 100g light cream cheese spread.

Tuna Pasta Bake

SERVES 6

530
KCAL

32g
PROTEIN

PER PORTION

If you're trying to avoid unnecessary trips to the shops, you'll probably already have the four main ingredients for this in your cupboard and you can throw it together in under half an hour. Simple, cost-effective and nourishing.

600g **dried short pasta**

3 x 145g tins **tuna**, drained

200g tin **sweetcorn**, drained

200g bag **spinach**, chopped

1 tbsp **dried parsley**

salt and **pepper**

100ml **low-fat milk**

200ml **Hellmann's Lighter than Light Mayonnaise**

80g **light Cheddar cheese**, grated

1. Preheat the oven to 190°C/170°C fan/gas mark 5.

2. Cook the pasta according to the instructions on the packet, drain and set aside.

3. In a large bowl mix together the tuna, sweetcorn, spinach, parsley, salt, pepper, milk and mayonnaise.

4. Add the cooked pasta to the dish and mix everything together.

5. Transfer to a large ovenproof dish. Sprinkle the cheese on top, cover with tinfoil and cook in the oven for 15 minutes until the cheese is melted.

6. This can be served cold or warm and it will keep in the fridge, covered, for a few days.

Gyros

SERVES 6

430 KCAL

33g PROTEIN

PER PORTION

This is a great one for the family to enjoy together, especially in the summer when you want a delicious but easy spread. It can be prepped the night or morning before you want to serve it. Then all you need to do is cook the chips and chop up some veggies and everyone can help themselves and build their own gyros. I would recommend serving my homemade tzatziki with it.

400g 5%-fat **pork mince**

2 **garlic cloves**, minced

1 tsp **ground cumin**

1 tsp **ground coriander**

1 tsp **onion powder**

½ tsp **smoked paprika**

½ tsp **sea salt**

½ tsp **ground black pepper**

4 **potatoes**, peeled and cut into chips

low-calorie spray cooking oil

6 **flatbreads** or **pittas**

½ head of **lettuce**, shredded

3 **tomatoes**, sliced

1 **red onion**, sliced

tzatziki (see page 270), to serve

1. Put the mince, garlic, cumin, coriander, onion powder, paprika, salt and pepper in a large bowl and mix together.

2. Mould the mixture into a large sausage shape and roll up tightly in tinfoil, making sure it's completely sealed. Leave it in the fridge for at least 4 hours or overnight.

3. Preheat the oven to 180°C/160°C fan/gas mark 4. If using an air fryer, preheat it (for about 3 minutes) to 180°C. Cook the gyros, with the tinfoil still on, for about 45 minutes.

4. Meanwhile, put the potatoes in a large microwave-safe bowl and microwave on high (800W) for 5 minutes. Spray with oil and spread them out on a large baking tray and cook for 30 to 40 minutes until crispy.

5. Then take the gyros out of the oven, leave to cool for 5 minutes, remove the tinfoil and slice thinly.

6. Warm your flatbreads or pittas for a few minutes in the oven. Add some of the sliced meat, homemade chips, shredded lettuce, sliced tomatoes and onion and a decent dollop of homemade tzatziki. Roll it up and enjoy.

I have always been a condiment connoisseur. My friends would call me the Garlic Sauce Queen! I honestly think I'd sometimes have more sauce on my plate than anything else! Having a delicious sauce to complement your meal can take your plate from an 8 to a 10. I never gave up on my sauces or sides throughout my journey – I just found ways to recreate them with simple, fresher and healthier ingredients.

Sauces & Sides

Crispy Kale & Chilli

SERVES 4

79
KCAL

1.6g
PROTEIN

PER PORTION

I know this sounds like one of the most boring sides imaginable, but once you've tried it you will see why so many people love it and why I've included it here. I would almost say it's addictive! Even better, kale is packed with vitamins and goodness.

200g **kale**

2 tbsp **olive oil**

1 tsp **chilli flakes**

1 tsp **sea salt**

1. Preheat the oven to 190°C/170°C fan/gas mark 5. If using an air fryer, preheat it (for about 3 minutes) to 190°C.

2. Mix all the ingredients in a large bowl, making sure the kale is completely covered with the oil.

3. Line a baking tray with baking paper and spread the kale on the tray.

4. Cook in the oven for 5–10 minutes, depending on how crisp you want it, tossing regularly.

JEN'S FAVOURITE

Homemade Chips

SERVES 4

154 KCAL

4g PROTEIN

PER PORTION

4 large **potatoes**, peeled and cut into chips

low-calorie spray cooking oil

salt, to taste

1. Preheat the oven to 190°C/170°C fan/gas mark 5. If using an air fryer, preheat it (for about 3 minutes) to 190°C.

2. Put the potatoes in a microwave-safe bowl, with no water or oil, and microwave on high (800W) for 5 minutes. Give them a good shake halfway through.

3. When they are ready you can drop them into some ice-cold water to remove some of the starch, which helps make them crispier (the longer you can leave them, the better).

4. Remove them from the water and pat dry. Spray evenly with some low-calorie spray oil and a little sea salt.

5. Cook them in the air fryer or oven for approximately 30 minutes until golden-brown, giving them a shake every so often to make sure they cook evenly.

Cauliflower Rice

52 **4g**

KCAL   PROTEIN

Making cauliflower rice at home is very easy. All you need is either a cheese grater or a food processor – a food processor makes it much quicker.

1 large head **cauliflower**

low-calorie spray cooking oil

1. Cut your cauliflower into medium-sized florets and grate it or blitz it in a food processor.

2. Cook the cauliflower rice in a little spray oil on the pan over a low medium heat for 3 to 5 minutes.

TIP

When cooking from frozen, microwave for 4 to 5 minutes at 800W.

Crispy Corn on the Cob

SERVES 4   CHIPOTLE MAYO

178 KCAL   **4.5g** PROTEIN

50 KCAL

Corn on the cob 'ribs' are having a real moment and I absolutely love them. They're so easy to make and you can use any spices you like. I like them with chipotle mayo and some feta cheese crumbled over then. Perfect for family barbecues – or just an entire bowl for yourself.

2 tbsp **olive oil**

½ tsp **chilli powder**

½ tsp **paprika**

½ tsp **garlic salt**

½ tsp **southern fried chicken seasoning** (Schwartz do a good one)

pinch of **salt** and **pepper**

4 **mini corn on the cobs** (quartered lengthwise to make 16 pieces)

30g **feta cheese**, crumbled

1 tsp **fresh chives**, finely chopped

For the chipotle mayo

4 tbsp **Hellman's Lighter than Light mayonnaise**

juice of ½ **lime**

1 tsp **chipotle flakes** (or **chilli flakes**)

½ tsp **buffalo seasoning**

pinch of **salt**

1. Preheat the oven to 200°C/180°C fan/ gas mark 6. If using an air fryer, preheat it (for about 3 minutes) to 200°C.

2. Mix together the olive oil, chilli powder, paprika, garlic salt, chicken seasoning and salt and pepper. Brush over each piece of corn.

3. Cook them, in two batches, in the air fryer or oven for 15 minutes, turning once.

4. For the chipotle mayo, mix all the ingredients together in a bowl until thoroughly combined.

5. Put the corn cobs in a bowl and top with crumbled feta, the chipotle mayo and chives.

JEN'S FAVOURITE

Homemade Hummus

SERVES 4

90 KCAL   **6g** PROTEIN

PER SERVING

400g tin **chickpeas**

1 tbsp **peanut butter** (smooth or crunchy)

3 tbsp **aquafaba** (the liquid in the chickpea tin – just add more if you like it smoother)

½ **garlic clove**

salt, to taste

squeeze of **lemon**

1. Drain and rinse the chickpeas, retaining the aquafaba.

2. Throw everything in a blender and blend until smooth.

Spicy Roast Red Pepper Hummus

SERVES 4

104
KCAL

6g
PROTEIN

PER SERVING

This is delicious served with warm bread, toasted pitta or salads. It is so easy to make and will keep for three or four days in the fridge.

low-calorie spray cooking oil

1 red bell pepper, quartered and seeds removed

400g tin **chickpeas**

1 garlic clove

3 tbsp **aquafaba** (the liquid in the chickpea tin)

1 tbsp **nut butter**

1 tsp **lemon juice**

1 tsp **smoked paprika**

salt, to taste

½ tsp **chipotle flakes** or **chilli flakes**

fresh parsley, chopped, to garnish

1. Preheat the oven to 190°C/170°C fan/gas mark 5.

2. Roast the red pepper in some spray oil for about 10 to 15 minutes until soft. Remove from the oven and allow to cool.

3. Drain and rinse the chickpeas, but keep the aquafaba.

4. Put the chickpeas, garlic, nut butter, aquafaba, lemon juice, smoked paprika, salt and roasted pepper into a blender and blend until smooth. Add more aquafaba if needed.

5. Transfer to a bowl and stir through the chipotle or chilli flakes. Garnish with some fresh parsley.

Barbecue Sauce

SERVES 12

28
KCAL

0.7g
PROTEIN

PER SERVING

This is perfect for slow-cooker dinners, or you can blend it smooth and use it as a dip. You can throw it on anything and everything or use it as a marinade.

low-calorie spray cooking oil

1 **onion**, finely chopped

2 **garlic cloves**, finely chopped

500ml carton **passata**

2 tbsp **apple cider vinegar** (or **balsamic vinegar**)

2 tbsp **tomato purée**

1–2 tbsp **honey**, according to taste

1 tbsp **Worcestershire sauce**

1 tsp **Dijon mustard**

1 tbsp **smoked paprika**

½–1 tsp **cayenne pepper**

salt and **pepper**

1. Soften the onion in some low-calorie spray oil on a large pan. After a few minutes add the garlic and cook on a low heat for 5 minutes.

2. Add the remaining ingredients, bring to the boil and allow to boil for a few minutes, stirring constantly. Then reduce the heat to low and simmer for 20 minutes.

3. Once it has cooled down completely, blend it until smooth and store in an airtight jar in the fridge. It will keep for up to two weeks.

Peppercorn Sauce

56
KCAL

5g
PROTEIN

PER SERVING

This is one of my favourites. I love peppercorn sauce with anything, not just steak. This has only six ingredients and it takes five minutes to whip up.

4 **mushrooms**, chopped

½ **onion**, chopped

low-calorie spray cooking oil

1 **beef stock cube**

1–2 tsp **whole black peppercorns** (depending on how peppery you like it!)

100g **fat-free natural yoghurt**

1. Fry off the chopped mushrooms and onion in some spray oil until soft and lightly browned.

2. Put the stock cube, peppercorns and the mushrooms and onion in a blender with 200ml warm water. Blend everything together to a smooth consistency.

3. Pour into a jug and stir in the yoghurt. Use more or less yoghurt according to your desired flavour and consistency.

TIP

This is best used on the day it's made, but I have kept it in the fridge for up to three days. When I want to use it, I heat a small amount in the microwave on low for 30 seconds, then stir it, heat again for 30 seconds and stir, and keep repeating until it is hot. This helps to prevent it curdling.

Coleslaw

SERVES 6

45
KCAL

1.5g
PROTEIN

PER SERVING

The perfect side to so many dinners. This recipe is great, especially in summer. You throw all the ingredients into a bowl, mix it up and everyone can help themselves to it. It's also handy for adding to sandwiches and salads and is so nice with a barbecued meal or in a burger. It will keep for three or four days in the fridge.

120g **Hellman's Lighter than Light mayonnaise**

80g **fat-free natural yoghurt**

2 tbsp **white vinegar**

¼ **white cabbage**, thinly sliced

1 **onion**, thinly sliced

1 **carrot**, grated

1 tbsp **fresh chives**, finely chopped

2 tsp **dried parsley**

1 tsp **mustard powder**

½ tsp **onion granules**

salt and **pepper**, to taste

1–2 tsp **sweetener** (optional)

Simply throw the ingredients in a bowl and mix it up!

Burger Sauce

24
KCAL

0.7g
PROTEIN

PER SERVING

This is such a handy sauce to have in the fridge. It's so good on a cheeseburger, but it's lovely with some crackers and cheese too.

low-calorie spray cooking oil

1 **onion**, chopped

1 tsp **chilli powder**

250ml **passata**

4 tbsp **balsamic vinegar**

2 tbsp **sweetener**

1 tbsp **Worcestershire sauce**

1 tsp **mustard**

½ tsp **paprika**

½ tsp **onion powder**

1. In a pan, cook the chopped onion in some low-calorie spray oil with the chilli powder over a medium heat, stirring constantly, for 5 minutes or until the onion is soft.

2. Add the rest of the ingredients, bring to the boil and then simmer for a few minutes, stirring continuously.

3. Remove from the heat and allow to cool. When it's cooled, transfer to an airtight jar. It will keep in the fridge for up to two weeks.

Super Easy Sauces

Here's a selection of my easiest sauces, dressings and dips – you can whip these up in minutes to transform your meals. Just add the ingredients to a bowl, give it a good stir and go!

Taco Sauce

SERVES 2

32 KCAL   **1g** PROTEIN

PER SERVING

3 tbsp **reduced-sugar tomato ketchup**

3 tbsp **Hellman's Lighter than Light mayonnaise**

2 tbsp **fat-free Greek yoghurt**

1 tsp **cayenne pepper**

1 **garlic clove**, minced

salt and **pepper**, to taste

Tartare Sauce

SERVES 2

23 KCAL   **1.1g** PROTEIN

PER SERVING

3 tbsp **Hellmann's Lighter than Light mayonnaise**

3 tbsp **fat-free Greek yoghurt**

juice of ½ **lemon**

1–2 tsp **capers**, chopped

1 tsp **dried dill**, finely chopped

1 tsp **dried parsley**, finely chopped

salt and **pepper**, to taste

Caesar Dressing

SERVES 2

54 KCAL   **4.3g** PROTEIN

PER SERVING

60g **natural yoghurt**

3 tbsp **Hellmann's Lighter than Light mayonnaise**

1 tsp **Worcestershire sauce**

2 **anchovies**, finely chopped

½ **garlic clove**, minced

1 tsp grated **Parmesan**

½ tsp **mustard powder**

squeeze of **lemon juice**

black pepper, to taste

Salsa

SERVES 4

45 KCAL   **2g** PROTEIN

PER SERVING

4 **tomatoes**, finely chopped

1 small **onion**, finely chopped

2 **garlic cloves**, finely chopped

a few **pickled jalapeños**, finely
chopped, to taste

1 tsp **fresh tarragon**, finely
chopped

1 tsp **fresh parsley**, finely
chopped

1 tsp **sea salt**, to taste

juice of ½ **lime**

1 tsp **honey** or **sweetener**

Garlic Sauce

SERVES 2

35
KCAL

2.2g
PROTEIN

PER SERVING

3 tbsp **Hellmann's Lighter than Light mayonnaise**

4 tbsp **fat-free natural yoghurt**

1 **garlic clove**, minced

1 tsp **fresh dill**, finely chopped

1 tsp **fresh chives**, finely chopped

pinch of **onion salt**

½ tsp **mustard powder** or **ground white pepper**

JEN'S FAVOURITE

Tzatziki

27 KCAL   **4.5g** PROTEIN

PER SERVING

280g **fat-free Greek yoghurt**
½ **cucumber**, grated (squeeze out
as much water as you can)
1 **garlic clove**, minced
1 tbsp **dried mint**
1 tbsp **fresh dill**, finely chopped
juice and zest of ½ **lemon**
salt and **pepper**, to taste

Acknowledgements

The list of people who have helped and supported me, not only with this book but also through the last few years of my journey, would be very long. I am so lucky and grateful to be able to say that, because I have had an overwhelming amount of support behind me.

Firstly, I would like to thank you, the reader, for taking the time to read my story and hopefully cook up a few of the recipes I have put together. It has not been easy to open up and share such a big part of my life, which I had kept hidden for so long. But I felt that if I was going to write a book it was important to be as open and as honest as I could be, with both myself and, of course, you. Thank you for allowing me to share my story with you.

To everyone who has supported my Instagram page, @jens_journey_ie. Lots of you have followed my page from the beginning and have shared your own stories and struggles with me, and for that, I am beyond grateful. I created a safe space online for myself, where I was able to connect with people who have been through similar things to me, and I felt far less alone when you shared your stories with me. It allowed me to feel comfortable and confident opening up more and more about my own personal struggles. Thank you to every single person who has ever contacted me, shown me love and support or simply interacted with my posts. It means a great deal to me. So many people over the last while have come into my life and helped me in ways they might not even know, and I appreciate you all.

I want to acknowledge any person who has ever experienced or is experiencing any form of abuse. Know that you are never alone, even when you might feel like you are. Support is available in many forms, whether that's talking to a family member or friend in a safe environment or speaking to someone anonymously at a support centre – there are always people here to listen. Things can get better. Remember that it may be a part of who you are, but it does not define who you are.

I would like to say a big thank you to Saoirse Domestic Violence Services who were a great support to me when I moved home to Ireland. They listened to me, supported me and guided me when I needed it. They have given me the tools and information to help me support others. The work they do is incredible, as is the care and passion they put into their work.

A 'bigger than basic' thank you to everyone at my second home, Back2Basics. I am lucky to not only have the most supportive trainers, who have been by my side through my entire journey (fitness, food and basically my therapy too!) but also have the nicest bunch of supportive people surrounding me every single day that I train there. Seán, Moe, Shorty, Dean, Lewis, Lisa and all the gang – thank you for everything. I can't imagine life without my B2B people!

I would like to thank everyone at Gill Books who has been a part of this incredible opportunity. Thank you for your patience, your support and your understanding in allowing me to tell my journey just as I wanted. Thank you to all the creative team involved who have helped me to bring the recipes, pictures and layout of the book together exactly how I envisioned and also allowed me to stay true to myself!

I'm so lucky to have a bunch of amazing ladies behind me in my agency that are all equally as hardworking, encouraging and as crazy as you get! Thank you, Jess, for always having my back, listening to my (many) worries and always pushing me on – you wear your crown so well. And thank you to Lynn for allowing me to be the best Britney dancer there ever was. You are a very close second. You all have been such a massive part of all of this, and I am very grateful I've such a sound bunch at the Collaborations Agency.

To my parents and all my family and friends – you will never know how much your love and support helped me when I needed it most. I am so very grateful that I have a family I can lean on for anything. I appreciate and love you more than you know. Thank you to my best friends, who have stuck by me through thick and thin and were there for me when I needed you most – you know who are. I love that we have grown up together, and I feel so lucky to be surrounded by such incredible women. You all inspire me every single day.

And finally, to my Carter. You have carried me through my hardest times. You always managed to shed light on my darkest days with your perfect little face and smile. I know in my heart that I was supposed to be your mammy and you arrived just when you were supposed to! I love you so much and I am so proud of the kind, wild little boy you are. I always look forward to a tomorrow with you, today, tomorrow and always.

Recipe index